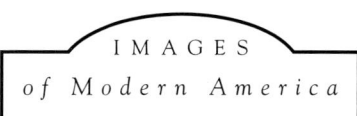

ATHENS

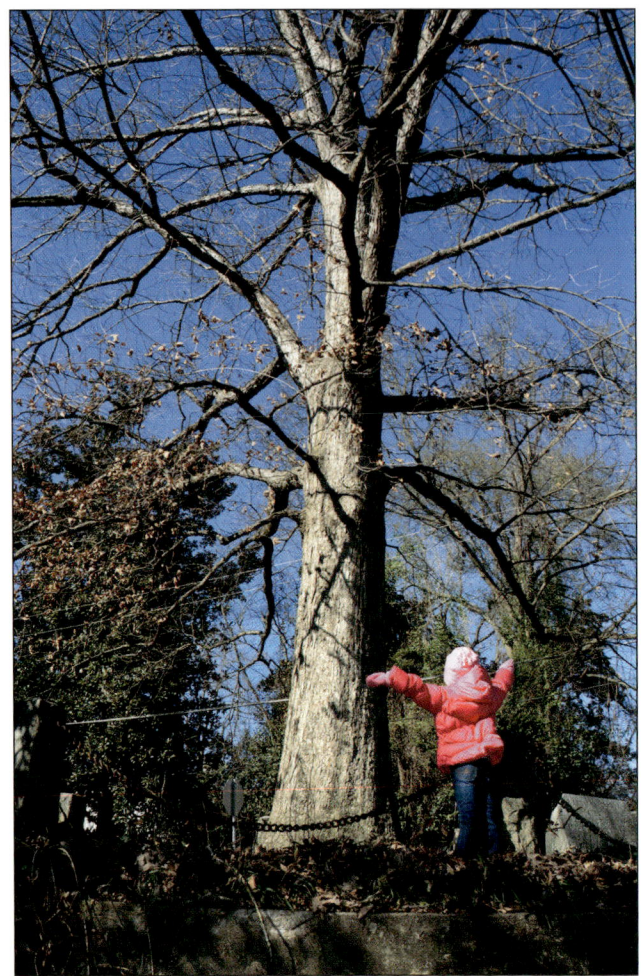

The "Tree That Owns Itself" is located on the corner of South Finley and Dearing Streets. Nearly 80 years after an article in the *Athens Banner* announced that Athens resident Col. William H. Jackson deeded a white oak tree to itself, becoming the Tree That Owns Itself, the legend was revealed to be a far-reaching myth. University of Georgia professor E. Merton Coulter's 1966 book, *The Toombs Oak, The Tree That Owned Itself, and Other Chapters of Georgia*, not only suggested that an inanimate object cannot legally own itself, but declared that there was never a deed presented by Jackson. The tree in this photograph is actually the son of the Tree That Owns Itself, as the original, 400-year-old decaying tree was toppled by a windstorm in 1942. The tree was designated as an Athens Historical Landmark in 1988. (Courtesy of McGinnis Leathers.)

On the Front Cover: Clockwise from top left: Epp Suddath, manager of the downtown Varsity for more than 40 years (see page 17); a student participating in the "Jesus movement" (see page 33); legendary University of Georgia running back Herschel Walker (see page 68); Widespread Panic playing on April 18, 1998 (see page 23); and Michael Stipe, lead singer of R.E.M. (see page 17).

On the Back Cover: Clockwise from top left: Georgia writer Lewis Grizzard (see page 71); Jason Aldean performing at Sanford Stadium (see page 95); and a young girl protests the Vietnam War in 1969 (see page 31).

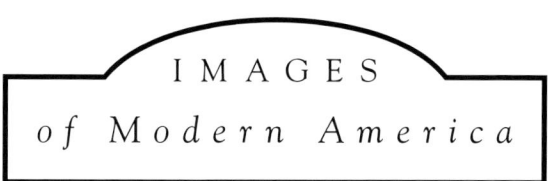

IMAGES
of Modern America

ATHENS

Patrick Garbin

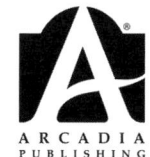

Copyright © 2014 by Patrick Garbin
ISBN 978-1-4671-1236-9

Published by Arcadia Publishing
Charleston, South Carolina

Printed in the United States of America

Library of Congress Control Number: 2014931544

For all general information, please contact Arcadia Publishing:
Telephone 843-853-2070
Fax 843-853-0044
E-mail sales@arcadiapublishing.com
For customer service and orders:
Toll-Free 1-888-313-2665

Visit us on the Internet at www.arcadiapublishing.com

To Elizabeth—a fellow Athens native and UGA graduate who, fortunately for me, became my wonderful and supportive wife

Contents

Acknowledgments		6
Introduction		7
1.	No Longer a Small, Sleepy College Town	9
2.	Student and Campus Life	27
3.	Historic Downtown	45
4.	How 'Bout Them Dogs?	61
5.	The Music Scene and Culture	79

Acknowledgments

From the onset of this project, my seventh traditionally published book, I discovered that as a writer and researcher, I was fairly unaccustomed to the book's subject matter and its unique editing and publishing process. Regardless, this wound up developing into one of my favorite book projects, and there are a number of individuals I need to acknowledge for making this unfamiliar-turned-highly-rewarding project a reality.

Photographs depicting Athens from the 1960s through the 1980s, especially those in color, are rather difficult to come by. Fortunately for me, the *Pandora*—the University of Georgia's student-run yearbook—has displayed images of the city beside those related to the university for the last several decades. I want to thank the *Pandora* staff, particularly editor-in-chief Molly Nicholson, for supplying more than half the photographs that appear in this book. Unless otherwise noted, all images appear courtesy of the *Pandora*. In addition, unless otherwise noted, all quoted material is from the University of Georgia's student newspaper, *The Red and Black*.

For this project, I was fortunate to work with three of the most distinguished photographers in the Athens/Atlanta area—McGinnis Leathers, Terry Allen, and Rob Saye—who each supplied a number of photographs for the book.

In addition, I want to recognize the other individuals and organizations that provided anywhere from one to a few images. In all, approximately 14 different sources supplied photographs for this project. I want to thank each and every one for not only their contributions to this book project, but for helping me realize, through their photographs, that there is plenty to discover regarding Athens's modern history beyond what I originally knew of this extraordinary city: George Suddath, Janice Henck, Dave Williams, Frank Platt, D.J. Pascale, Wayne Dean, Nigel Bynum, Helen Castronis, Ken Helms, Jerry Howell, the Office of Mayor Nancy Denson, Average Joes Entertainment, DariusGoesWest.org, and Spalding Entertainment.

Notably, this was my first book not solely about University of Georgia football and my first that was more of an image-finding project than one focused on writing. I would like to acknowledge Arcadia Publishing and particularly my editor, Liz Gurley. Thank you for allowing me to branch out, so to speak, as an author and for your patience and guidance throughout the entire process.

Finally, and above all, I want thank my wife, Elizabeth, and my two wonderful children, Trip and Rebecca. I appreciate your patience, as well, and your keen interest in this project. As residents of the Athens area, our enthusiasm for the Classic City made for a project we could enjoy together.

INTRODUCTION

The nickname of Athens, Georgia—the Classic City—can be traced back to the 1870s, when Athens was considered "classic" simply for its name and neoclassical architecture, while the "city" only contained around 5,000 residents at the time. The University of Georgia (UGA) was primarily responsible for the town's initial growth spurt, and by 1960 the population of Athens was six times that of a century before. Still, as late as 1957, although Athens was "trying so very hard to become a real city" according to an article from that year, it had "the attitudes and policies of a small country town. And without that sacrifice [of such attitudes and policies] it will always be nothing more than that."

This book is intended to be a pictorial "modern" history of Athens. It begins just past the time when life anatomy classes were literally not taught at UGA because the Athens "townspeople would frown upon them as 'choking and vulgar displays' " and follows the area's evolution into a thriving, diverse, unique city in which the original attitudes and policies were sacrificed over the course of the next 50-plus years.

A number of different subjects can be identified with Athens from the 1960s to the present, but only so many can be depicted on the following pages. After much consideration, plus asking the opinion of several other native Athenians, I have chosen overarching themes, each of which serves as a chapter in the book: student and campus life (predominantly at UGA), the businesses and attractions of the city's historic downtown district, the Georgia Bulldogs (UGA's athletic teams), and the unparalleled music scene and unique culture of Athens. Most prominently, and thus addressed in the first chapter in the book, is how much and how quickly Athens has changed during the last half-century—perhaps more so than any other college town in the country.

The extensive development of Athens began with the integration of area schools, first at UGA in 1961 and in the Clarke County public school system soon thereafter. In the early 1960s, Beechwood Shopping Center opened, the town's first shopping center. This is significant because after Beechwood's opening, many shopping centers followed over the next two decades—including the Georgia Square Mall, the county's first and only shopping mall—and forced many downtown retail stores to relocate into shopping centers or close their doors altogether. Instead of serving a common retail center, the downtown area of Athens was on the verge of becoming something much more extraordinary.

Like many college towns of the time, Athens had its fair share of demonstrators during the late 1960s and early 1970s: Vietnam War protests were followed by those supporting the women's liberation movement and those advocating for gay rights. In 1974, UGA students joined the unusual nationwide phenomenon of "streaking" (running in the nude). On March 7, 1974, more than 1,500 simultaneous streakers on the university campus set the world record for largest group streak—a record that still stands more than 40 years later. By the mid-1970s, the population of Athens had increased approximately 50 percent since 1960; in 1976, the growth was supported by the introduction of citywide public bus transportation: the Athens Transit System.

In a history about a town known for its party-like atmosphere, it would be remiss to not mention what has been called the wildest night in the history of Athens: the post-game celebration that followed the UGA football team's 21-0 upset victory over Alabama in 1976. Countless partiers invaded Milledge Avenue, causing the police to completely close the road from Broad Street to Five Points—a distance of more than a mile. Speaking of being festive, by the end of the 1970s, a foundation had been laid for the city's soon-to-be-celebrated music and art scene as bands like The B-52's, R.E.M., Widespread Panic, and other recognizable acts began to perform at places like the Georgia Theatre, 40 Watt Club, and Uptown Lounge.

For the 1980 season, the Bulldogs were the top team in all of college football after UGA won its first national title in any sport (the football team claims a "consensus" national championship for its 1942 season, but it was not recognized as such until the 1990s). After nearly a century of athletic competition but no national titles, the Bulldogs captured a combined 39 team national championships in nine different sports from 1980 through the 2013–2014 academic year, including 10 in women's gymnastics. The 1980s also saw the arrival of more music venues, bars, restaurants, artistic outlets, and coffee shops in Athens to cater to the city's creative climate.

In the early 1990s, Clarke County and the City of Athens unified their governments, becoming only the second unified government in the state (and the 28th in the nation); this caused the city's population to rise to over 100,000. In 1996, Athens hosted three sporting events for Atlanta's Summer Olympic Games. Two years later, the city was the site for the "world's largest record release party," when as many as 100,000 people crowded the streets of Athens for a free concert performed by hometown band Widespread Panic.

Throughout the 2000s, Athens has continued to grow and has much to offer both residents and visitors. Although the city has recently struggled with continuous growth and an unpredictable economy, some things, as they say, remain the same.

Athens's music and art scene still flourishes, and the half-dozen "football Saturdays" hosted by the Georgia Bulldogs in Sanford Stadium provide excitement for more than 90,000 spectators each autumn. Visitors and residents can enjoy the quiet and beauty of the State Botanical Garden of Georgia or the Georgia Museum of Art, while a couple of old landmarks—Athens's double-barreled cannon and the Tree That Owns Itself—continue to be cherished, and likely will be forever. As for the downtown district, it can now be described as something nearly every town and city in America desires: a 24-hour central area that contains varied shops, numerous restaurants and bars, and residents.

It is said that once you live in Athens, it can be a difficult place to leave behind. Personally, I can attest to this, as I was born and raised in the area and then attended the University of Georgia. Upon graduating, I reluctantly moved away. But, as the lyrics from R.E.M.'s song "Letter Never Sent" attest: "Vacation in Athens is calling me . . . Heaven's yours where I live." After a 14-year hiatus, I was fortunate to recently return to the Athens area. This time around, I plan on staying in the Classic City for good. Plus, with a family of my own, I now get to share the enjoyment of a place that is undoubtedly a real city—one that is "classic" in so many ways beyond its name and architecture.

One

NO LONGER A SMALL, SLEEPY COLLEGE TOWN

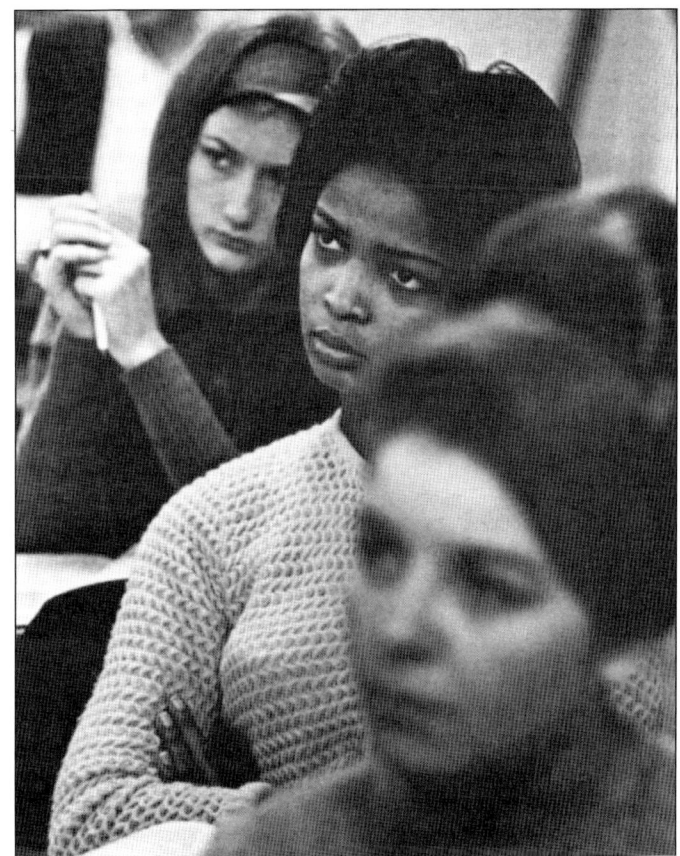

On January 9, 1961, Hamilton Holmes and Charlayne Hunter, who had both attended an all-black high school in Atlanta, desegregated the University of Georgia when they registered for classes, marking a defining moment in civil-rights history. Two years later, four African American girls—Wilucia Green, Margie Green, Agnes Green, and Bonnie Hampton—integrated Clarke County public schools under the "freedom of choice" plan.

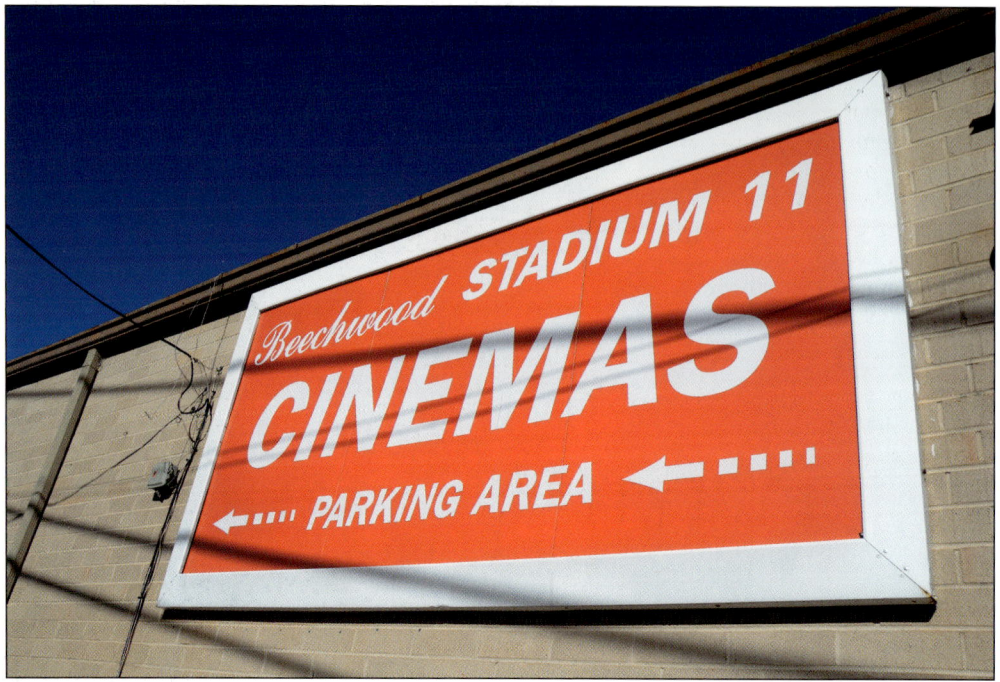

The Beechwood Shopping Center, the first shopping center in Athens, opened in the early 1960s. A few of the first businesses in the center included Henrietta's Beauty Shop, Cunningham Men's Wear, and Beechwood Cinemas. The movie theater, which is still in business after more than 50 years, was initially operated by Sol Abrams, president of Beechwood Enterprises, Inc. (Courtesy of McGinnis Leathers.)

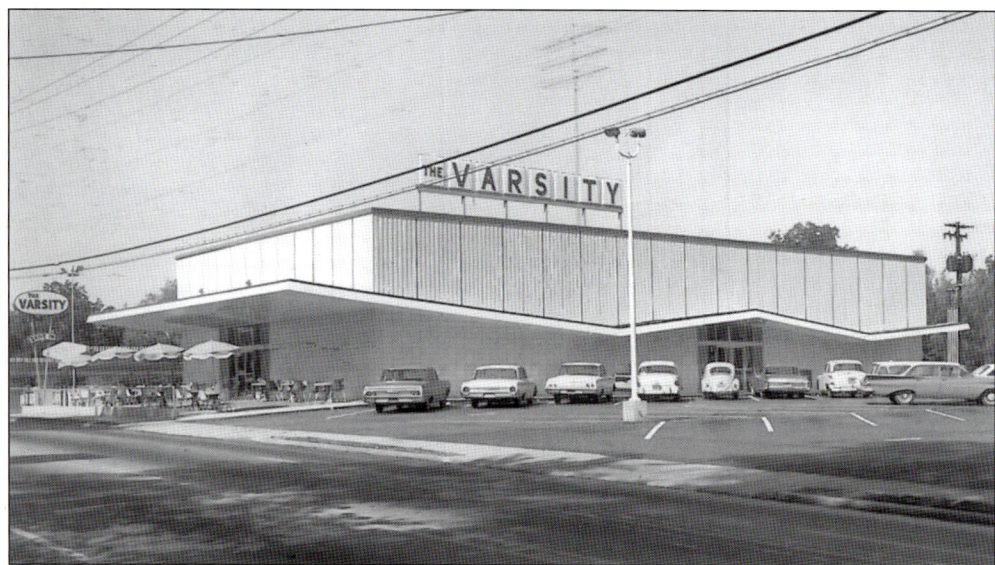

In 1964, The Varsity opened a second restaurant in Athens at 1000 West Broad Street, less than a mile from the original downtown Varsity at 101 College Avenue. The "new" Varsity, which recently celebrated its 50th anniversary, featured "Athens' largest, and most modern scientifically designed drive-in," according to the restaurant. (Courtesy of George Suddath, photograph by Kenneth Kay.)

In this mid-1960s image, Lumpkin Street seems just as crowded with people and automobiles as it is today. Of course, this photograph was taken immediately following a Georgia football game, which explains why the street is jam-packed. Around this time, both UGA enrollment and the Athens population were only about one third of what they are now.

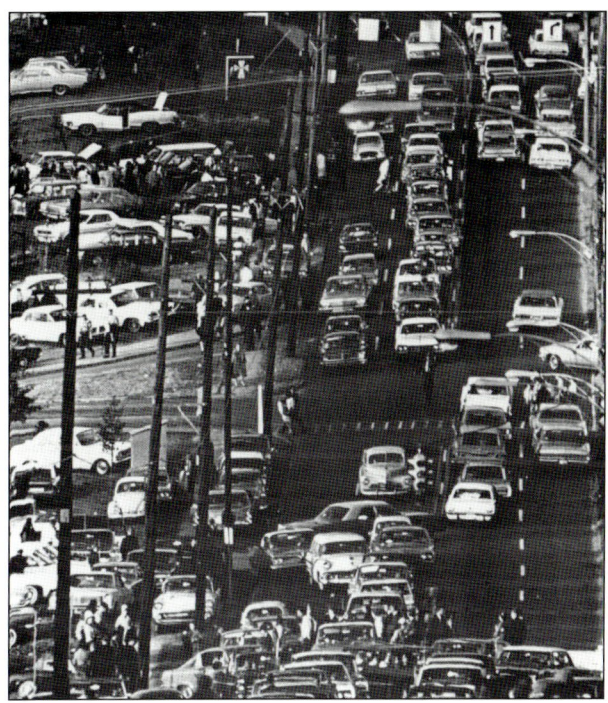

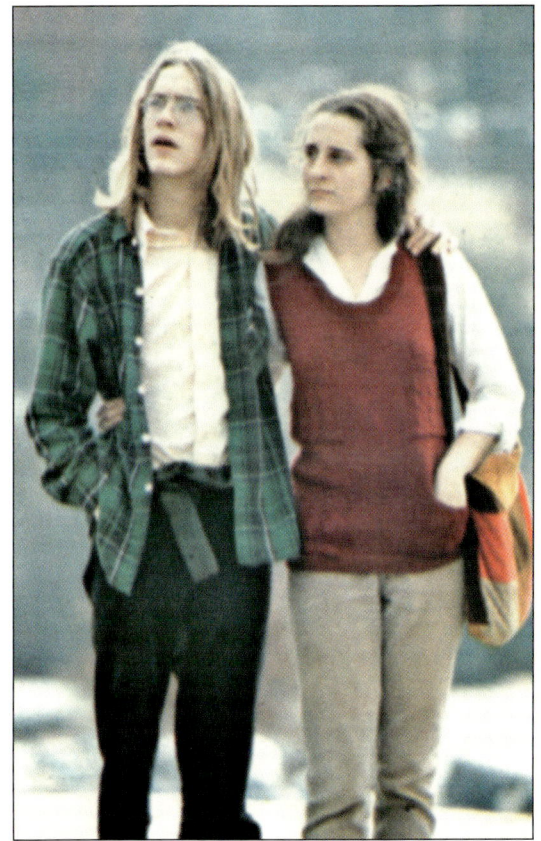

The 1960s featured drastic changes in the appearance of the nation's young people, as exhibited by this unidentified UGA student couple, and in sexual behavior. Opinions of local experts often differed concerning the era's "sexual revolution." For example, during the 1966–1967 academic year, M. Lindsey Cowan, UGA's dean of the law school, declared that such sexual behavior was nothing new but had always gone on, while Dr. Charles Darby, a professor of psychology, asserted that the revolution was more like an "evolution."

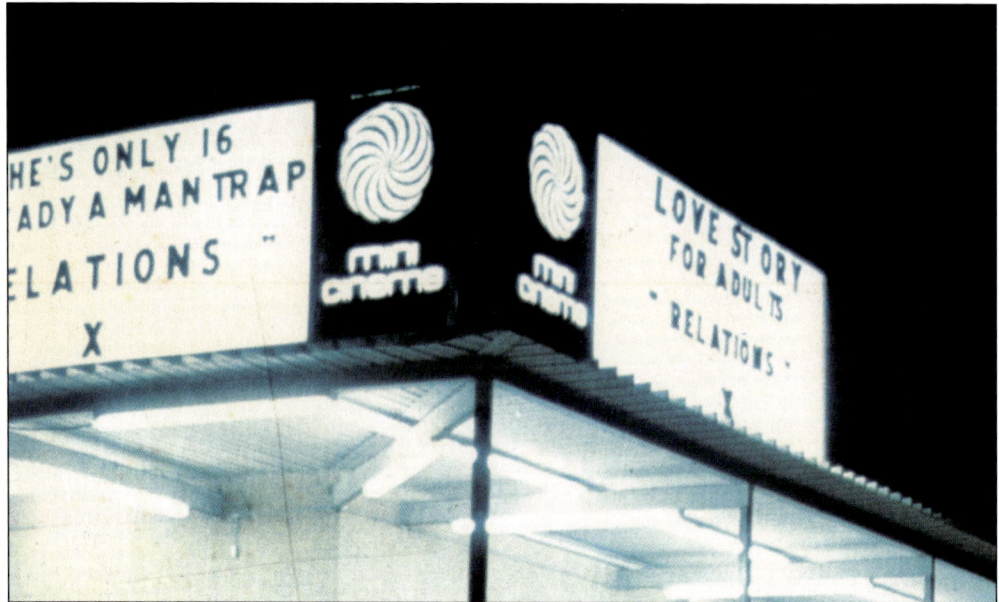

The Mini Cinema opened in 1968 on Alps Road across the street from the Beechwood Cinema. Since it only seated about 100 people, the Mini Cinema was minuscule compared to its counterpart. Although it eventually expanded to show a variety of films, the Mini Cinema initially specialized in adult movies.

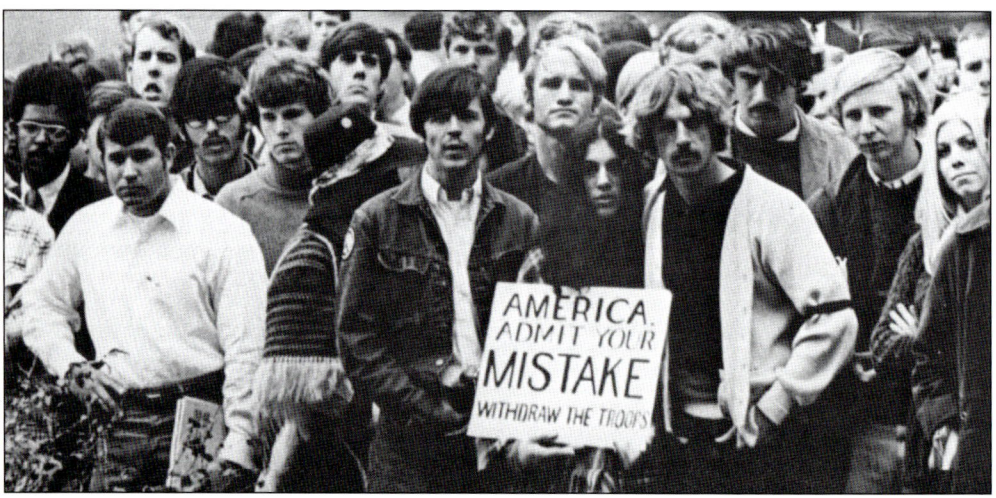

The University of Georgia's "Vietnam Moratorium," held on October 15, 1969, was a firm stand in protest against the United States' involvement in the Vietnam War; the demonstration was largely nonviolent. The day's activities included a memorial service held outside UGA's Memorial Hall, a performance by a vocal group (the Caledonian Mission), and prayers by local clergymen.

By the early 1970s, there had been a drastic change in the attire of UGA students. This was especially the case for the female population, some of whom, like the young lady in this photograph, seemingly wore hardly any clothes at all. This offered a sharp contrast to the time when the 1962–1963 UGA Student Handbook declared that women could not wear "Bermuda shorts and other sports attire" in public and that jackets had to be worn over backless dresses in classrooms.

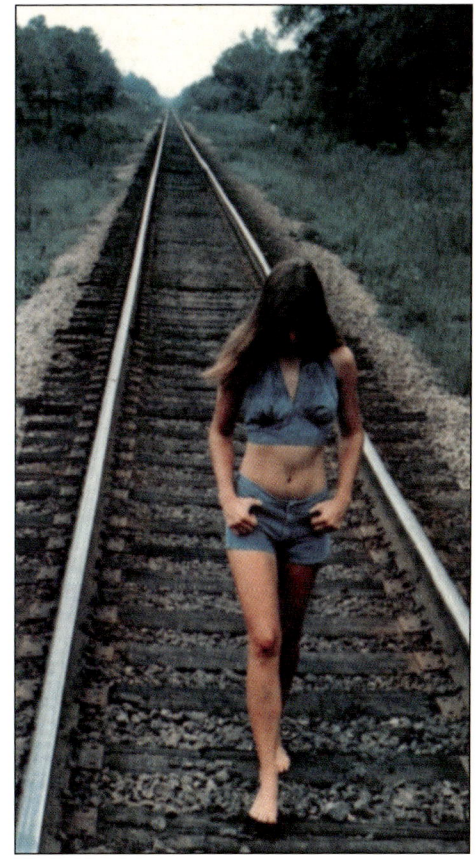

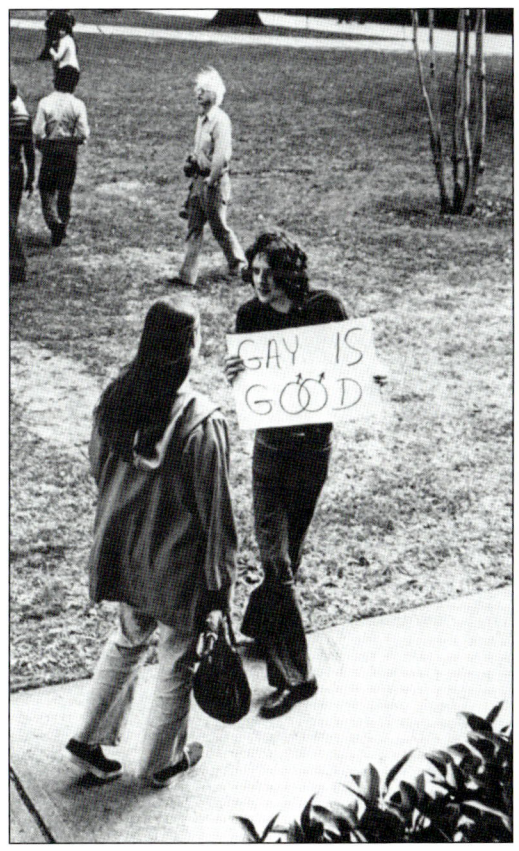

In 1971, what was believed to be the first homosexual activism in Athens took place when two UGA students—Bill Green and John Goard—appeared before a resident assistants' seminar group to declare that they were forming the Committee on Gay Education to bridge the "understanding between 'gay' people and 'straight' people."

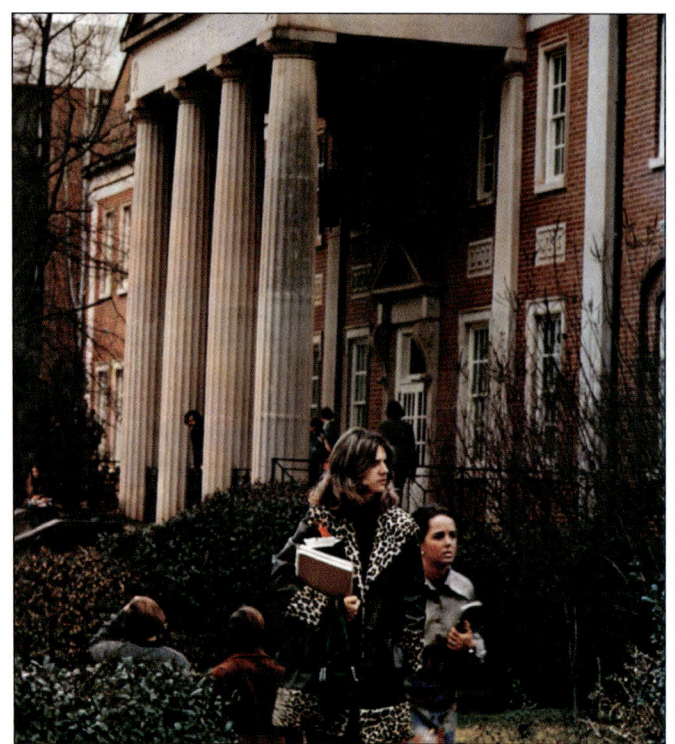

Women's liberation was another movement popular in Athens during the early 1970s, or around the time UGA's female population first made up at least 40 percent of all university students. The city's WOMEN (Women's Oppression Must End Now) organization, which mostly consisted of UGA students, emphasized "what sisterhood is all about—coming together to help other people as well as yourself."

In 1968, Athens and Clarke County residents voted "yes" to make the county "wet," allowing for the legal sale of alcoholic beverages. As shown in this 1972 photograph of Baxter Street, package (liquor) stores soon began to pop up throughout the area. Note the Budweiser and Brown Jug Package Store signs in the center of the photograph. At the time, another package store, Copper Kettle Package Store, was across the street.

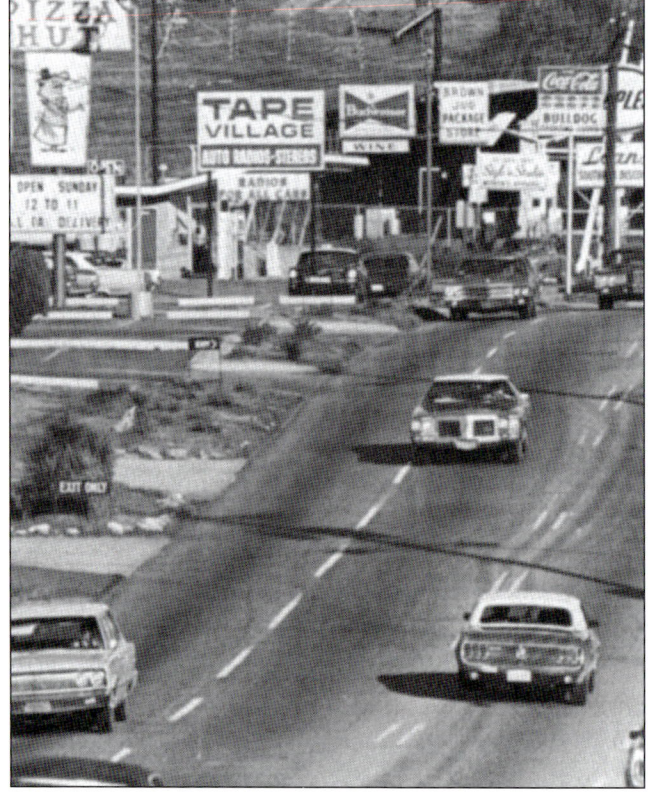

This image—merely part of a depiction of Effie's—was taken more than 20 years after the business closed in 1974. The legendary house of ill repute actually consisted of three houses located at 157, 165, and 175 Elm Street. After eight raids in 18 years, the three bordellos by the river were padlocked by Athens district attorney Harry Gordon on a charge of "public nuisance." (Courtesy of Terry Allen.)

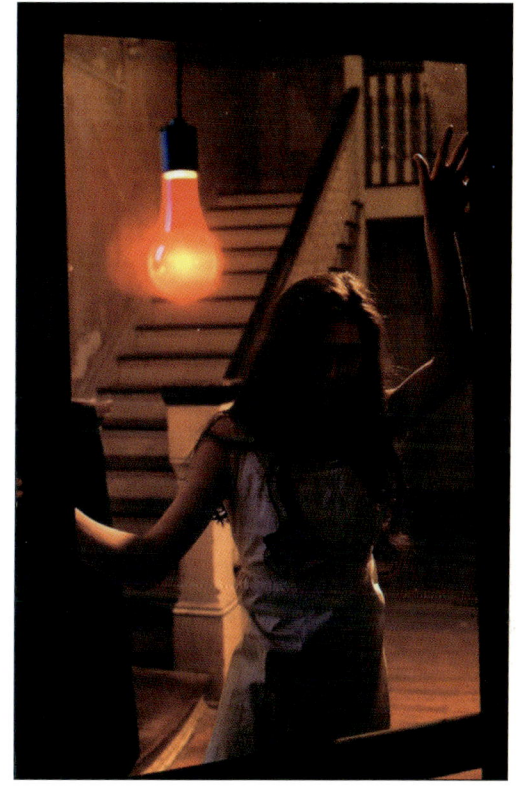

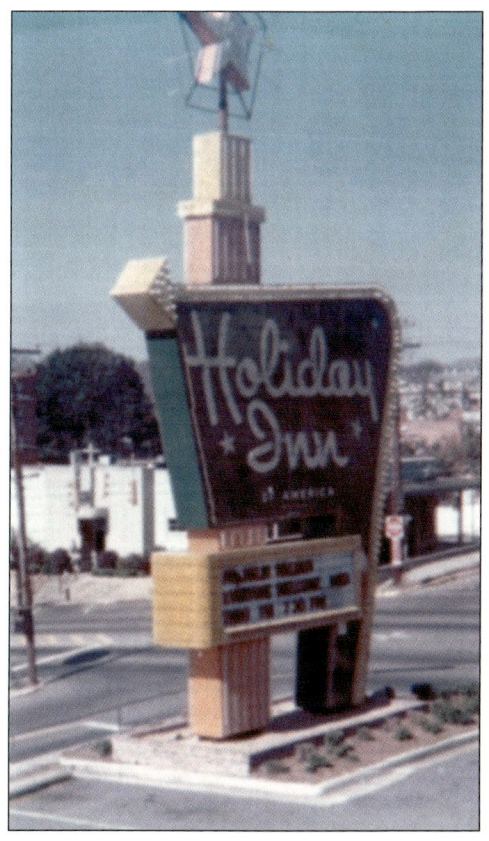

The Holiday Inn in downtown Athens, pictured here in 1976, is located on East Broad Street. It opened on September 15, 1960, as a courtyard motor lodge with less than 70 rooms. The hotel, which is now more than 50 years old and contains more than 200 guest rooms, is the oldest continuously running Holiday Inn franchise in North America. (Courtesy of Janice Henck.)

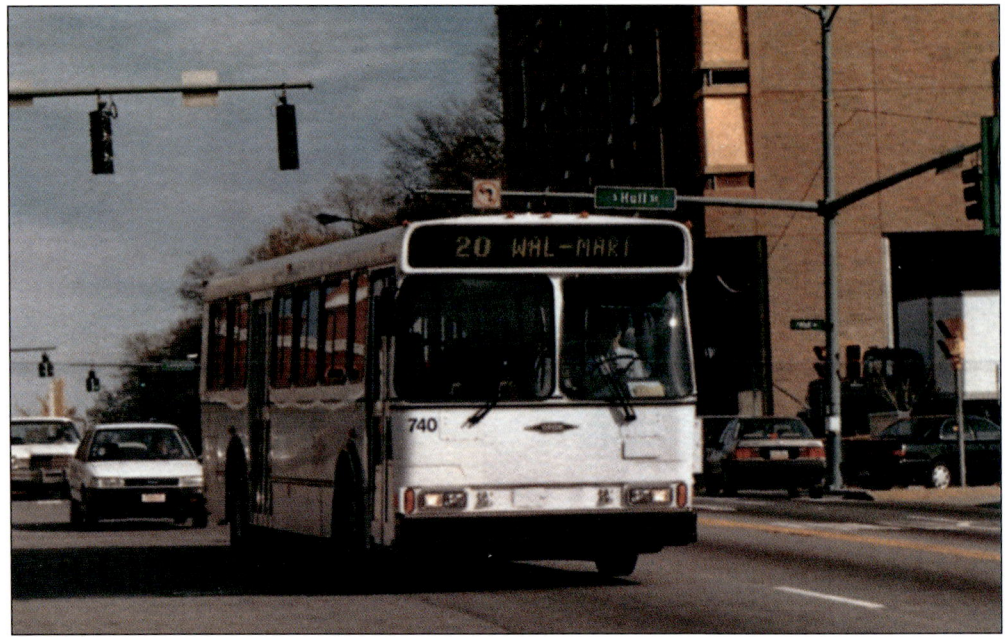

After voters approved a city-supported transit system in May 1973, the Athens Transit System (ATS) began operating on November 1, 1976. The initial system was supported by 16 new 43-passenger, $62,000 buses driven by 12 drivers. Originally, the ATS had eight routes and charged a fare of 25¢; today, it has 18 routes and charges a $1.60 fare for adults ages 18 to 64.

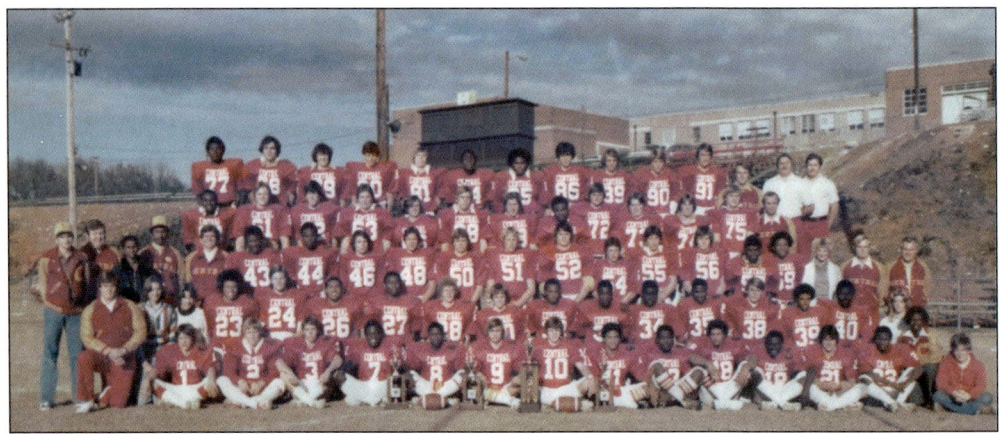

The first five Clarke Central High School football teams (from 1970 to 1974) did not make the playoffs, but the next 18 consecutive Gladiator squads (through 1992) reached the postseason under the direction of legendary head coach Billy Henderson (far right, third row). This is Clarke Central's 1977 state championship team. Henderson also coached state championship teams in 1979 and 1985. (Courtesy of Dave Williams.)

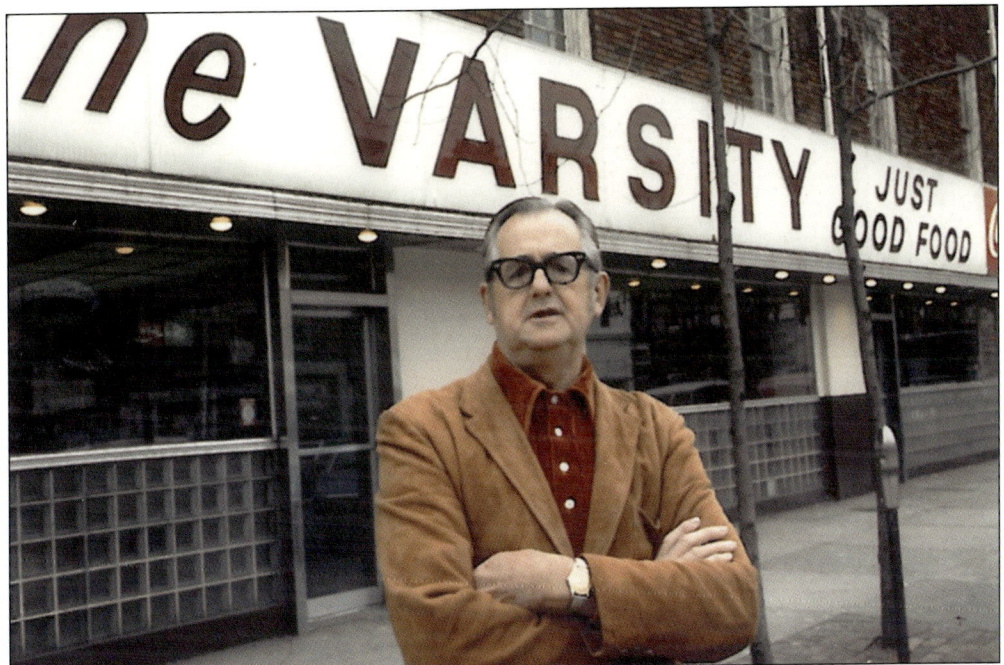

Epp Suddath stands in front of the downtown Varsity on December 20, 1978, the day the landmark restaurant closed its doors. Five years after his retirement, Suddath attended the restaurant's closing and met with other notable city residents, including Athens legislator Chappelle Matthews, UGA dean William Tate, and coach Mike Castronis, for "one last coffee break, a final chili dog and a moment of silence," according to the *Georgia Alumni Record*. (Courtesy of George Suddath.)

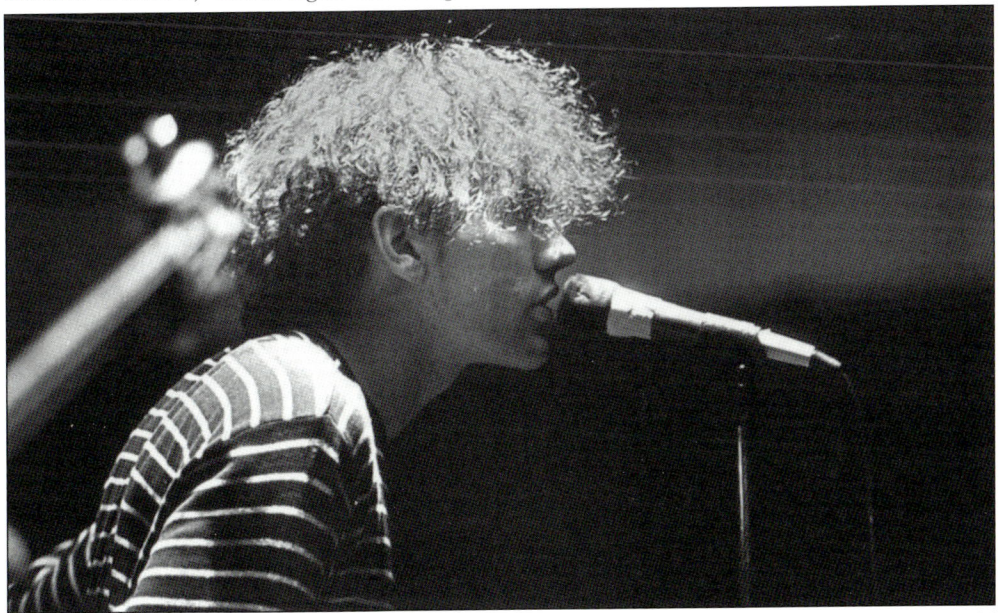

Michael Stipe, lead singer of R.E.M., performs in early October 1980 at Tyrone's O.C. ("Old Chameleon," the club's original name). At the time, the band had been performing together for less than a year but was on the verge of becoming one of the world's most popular rock acts. (Courtesy of Terry Allen.)

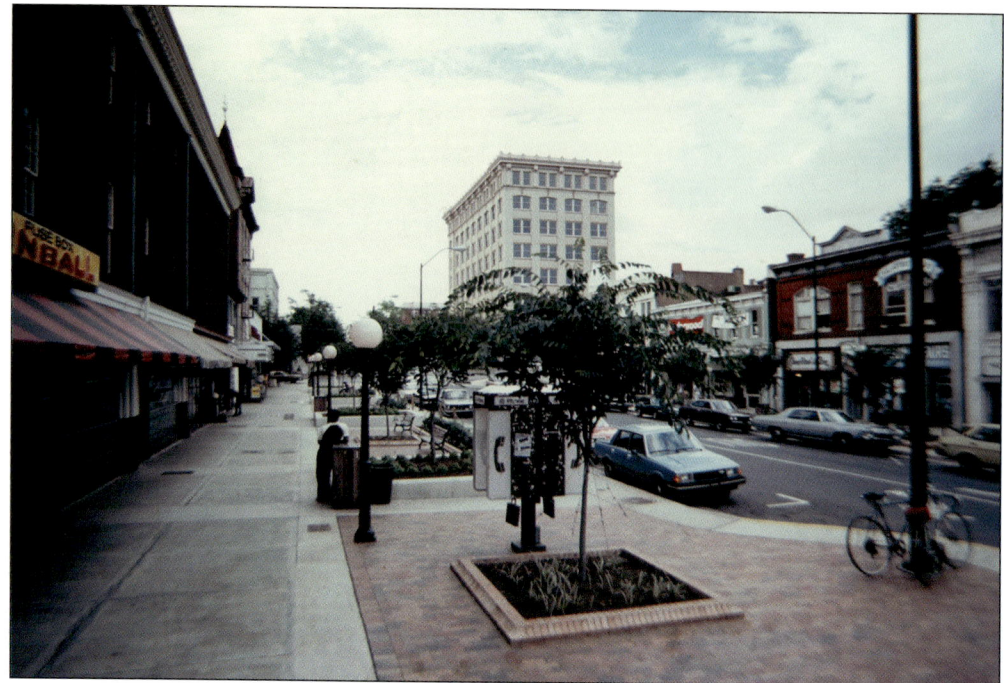

The businesses, automobiles, and heights of the trees may have changed, but these two images offer the exact same view of downtown—standing on Broad Street looking up College Avenue—separated by 33 years. In the 1980 photograph above, the corner of Broad and College Avenue was home to The Fuse Box, one of the biggest pinball companies in the nation at the time, which filled the space occupied by the original Varsity. Today, that spot is occupied by Five Guys, which, like the Varsity, is a burgers-and-fries restaurant. (Above, courtesy of Terry Allen; below, McGinnis Leathers.)

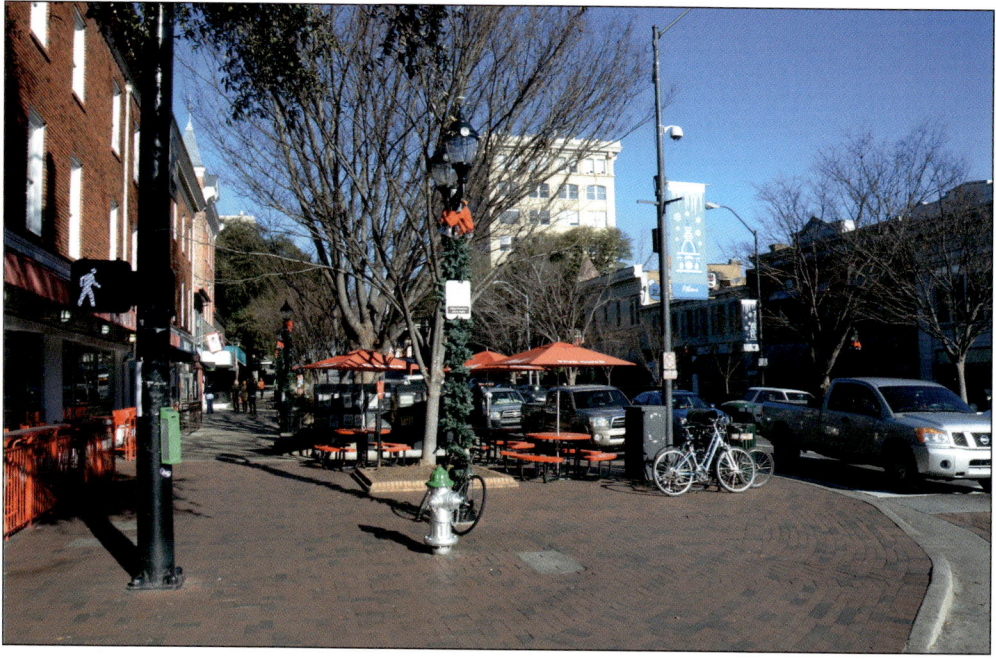

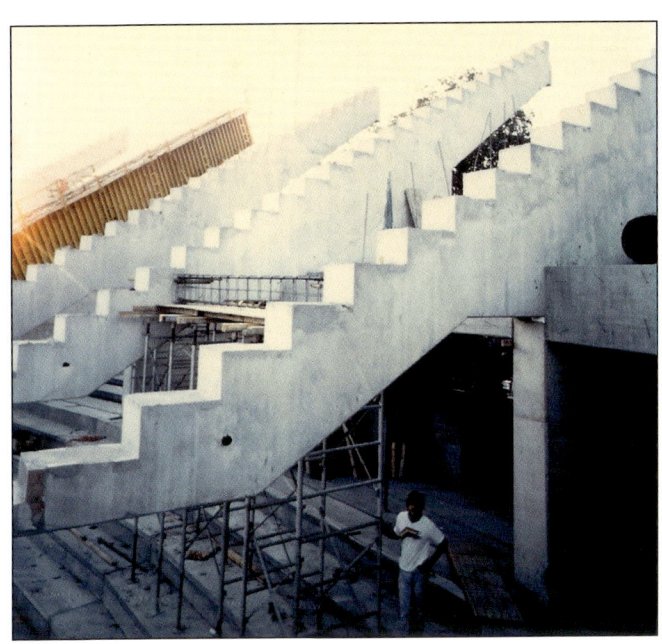

An unidentified construction worker—specifically, a waterproofer—poses in the summer of 1981 while working on the enclosure of Sanford Stadium's east end zone. The new addition was barely completed in time for the UGA football team's home opener against Tennessee on September 5. After the addition, the stadium's capacity increased from around 60,000 to over 80,000. (Courtesy of Rob Saye.)

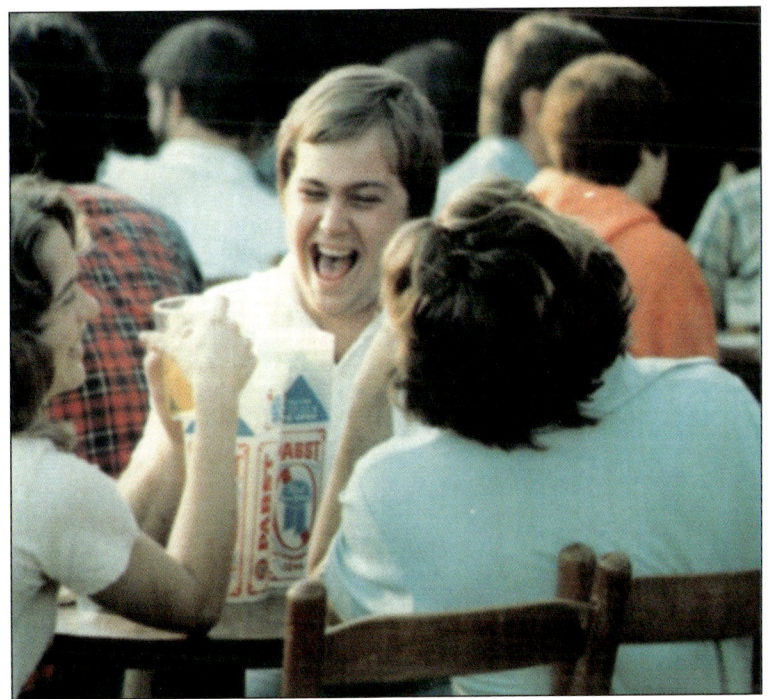

This 1980s image shows a group of unidentified people enjoying drinks at an Athens watering hole. The legal drinking age in the state of Georgia increased from 18 to 19 in 1980, from 19 to 20 in 1985, and finally from 20 to 21 in 1986. Raising the drinking age had a definite adverse affect on Athens nightclubs.

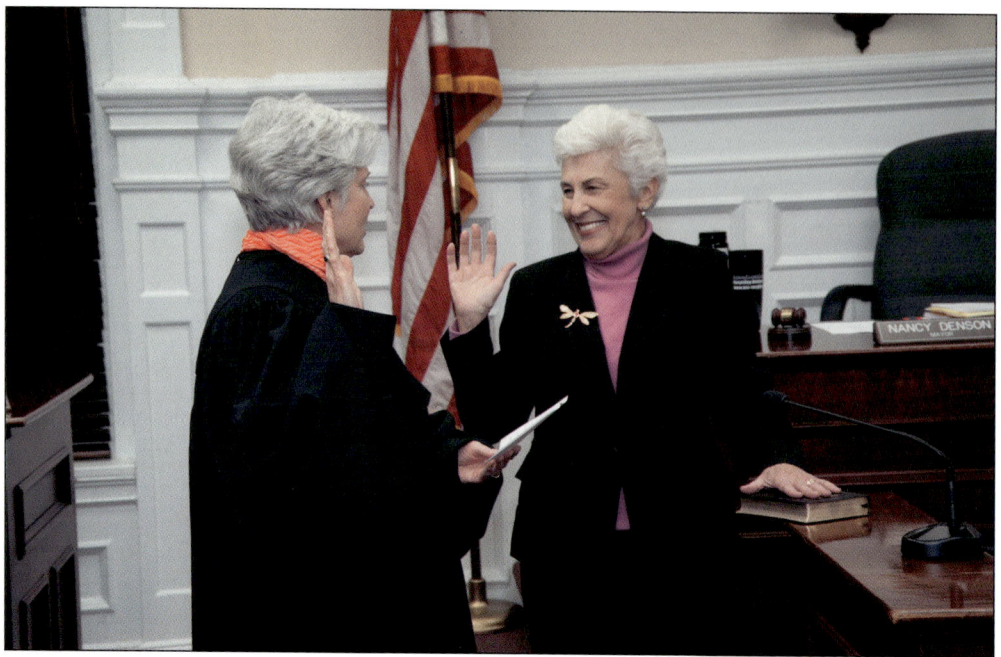

Shown here being sworn in as mayor of Athens on January 20, 2011, Nancy Denson (right) served the city as Clarke County tax commissioner from 1985 until she became mayor in 2011. In 1990, Athens and Clarke County consolidated to create a unified government, whereupon Denson continued serving as the tax commissioner of Athens-Clarke County. (Courtesy of the Office of Mayor Nancy Denson.)

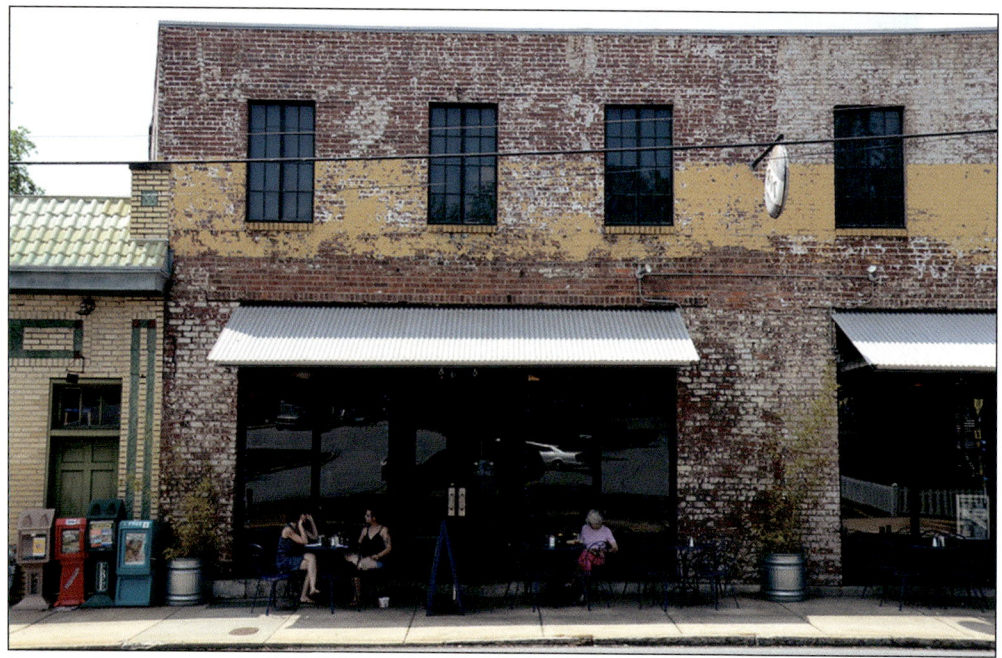

During the summer of 1990, The Grit moved from its Hoyt Street location to Prince Avenue, where it remains today. Besides being a vegetarian restaurant, The Grit was also a unique eatery for the time since it displayed works created by local artists. (Courtesy of McGinnis Leathers.)

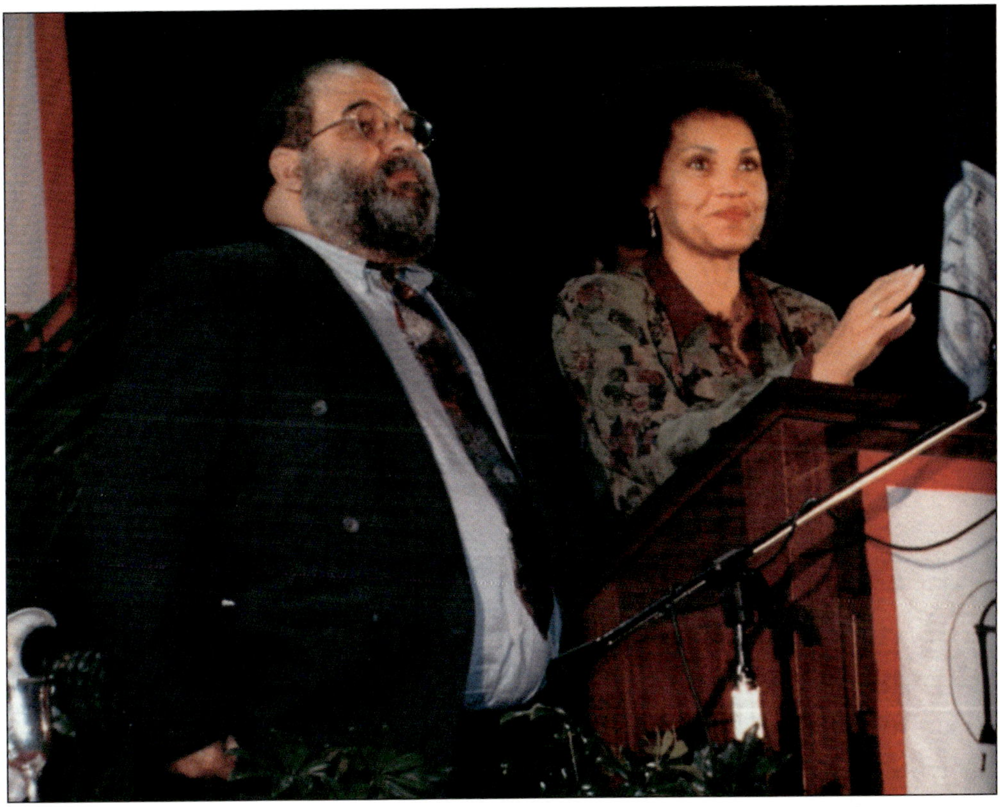

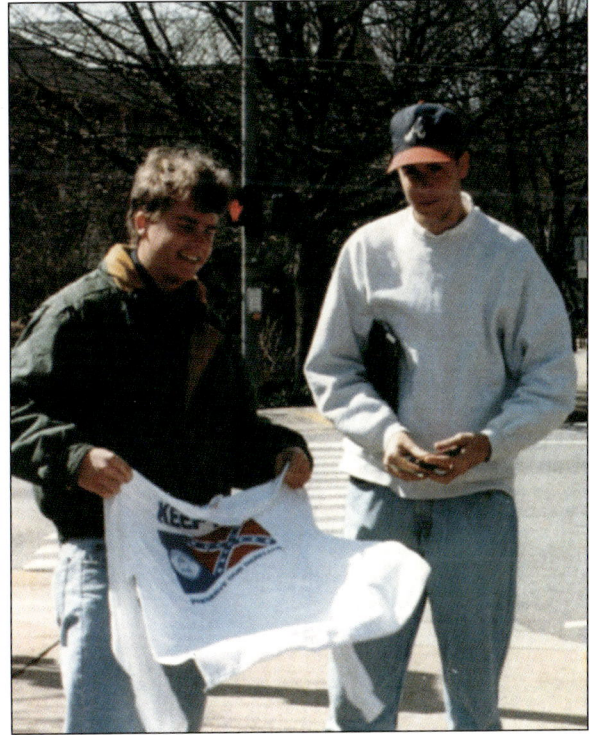

Dr. Hamilton Holmes and Charlayne Hunter-Gault, the first two African American students at UGA, are pictured attending the eighth annual Holmes-Hunter lecture on November 5, 1992. The 1992 lecture, given by Rev. Jesse Jackson in front of 3,500 people at the UGA Coliseum, was delivered nearly 32 years after Holmes and Hunter enrolled at the school as students.

In the 1990s, particularly leading up to the 1996 Olympics held in Atlanta, political pressure mounted to change the Georgia state flag because of the Confederate "stars and bars" that were on the flag at the time. This photograph shows Randy Meredith (left), who sold both "Keep It" and "Change It" Georgia state flag T-shirts on the UGA campus during the mid-1990s.

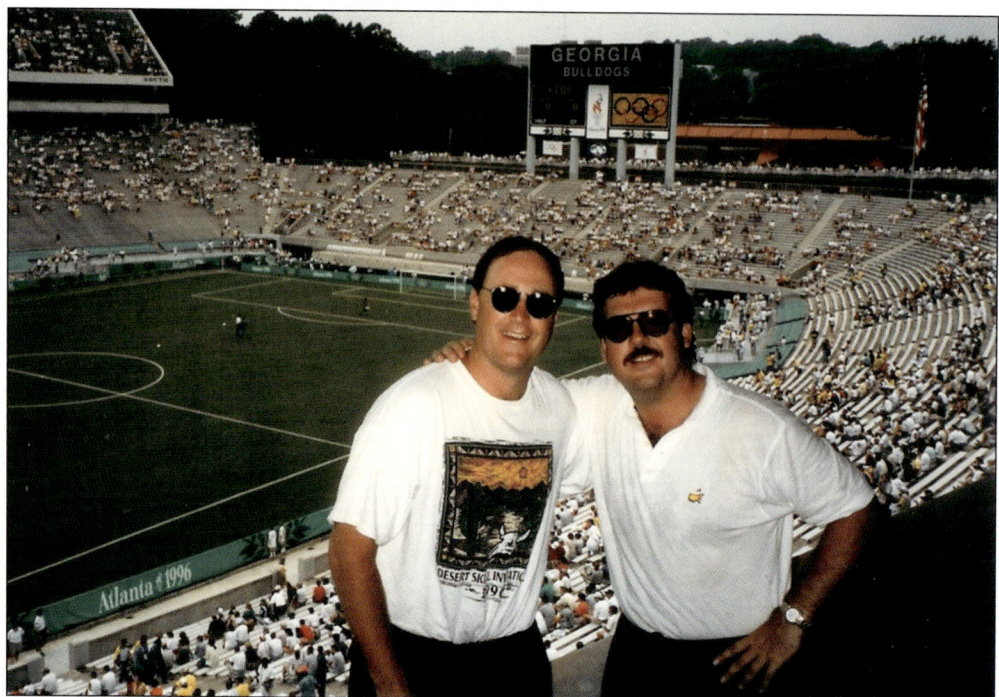

Friends Tracy Armstrong (left) and Rob Saye pose before to the start of a men's soccer semifinal match between Nigeria and Brazil on July 31, 1996, during the Summer Olympic Games. During the Olympics, Athens hosted soccer at Sanford Stadium and rhythmic gymnastics and indoor volleyball at Stegeman Coliseum. (Courtesy of Rob Saye.)

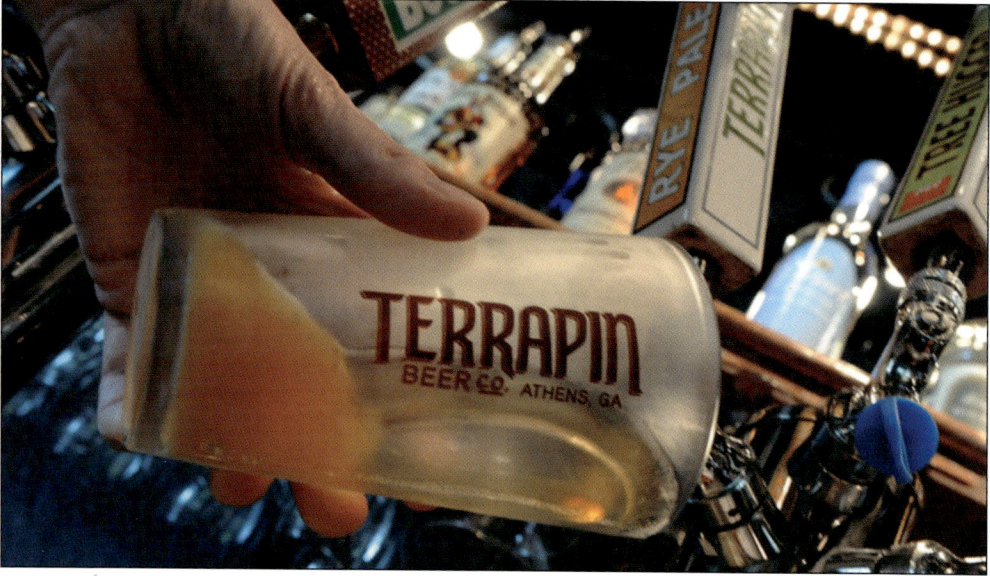

In 2002, Brian "Spike" Buckowski and John Cochran founded the Athens-based Terrapin Beer Company, which was named for the Grateful Dead album *Terrapin Station*. That same year, their Rye Pale Ale won the gold medal in the American-Style Pale Ale category at the Great American Beer Festival. The craft brewery is now housed in a 40,000-square-foot facility on Newton Bridge Road. (Courtesy of McGinnis Leathers.)

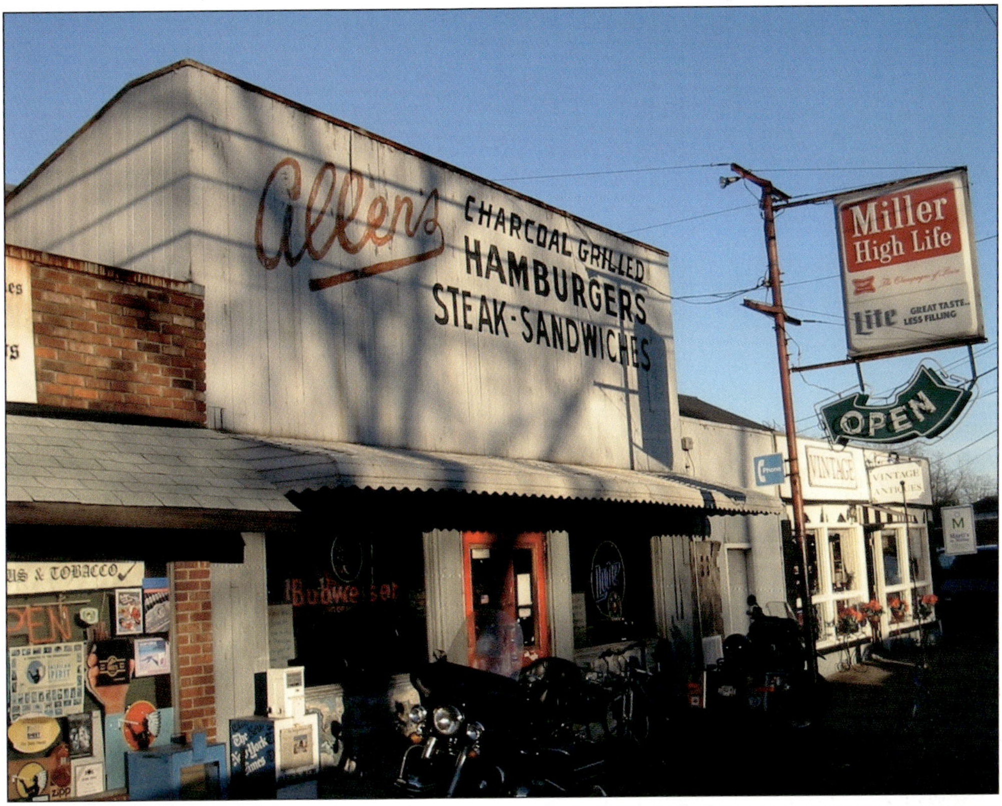

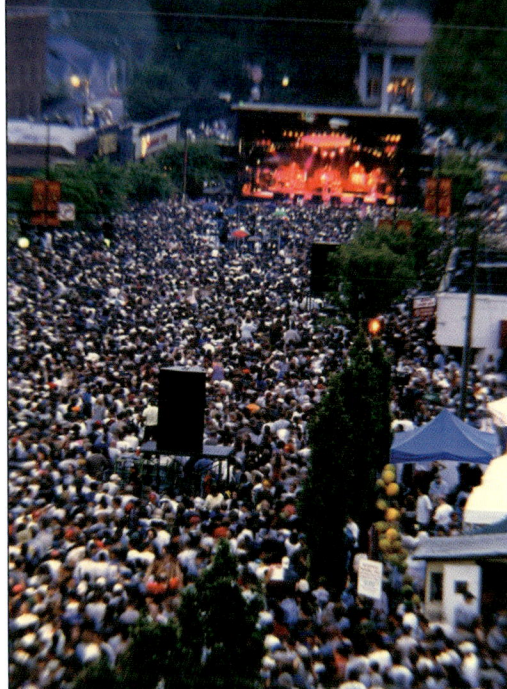

This photograph was taken on December 31, 2003, the final day of service at the original location of the acclaimed Allen's restaurant on Prince Avenue, which had been open for nearly 50 years. In 2007, Allen's reopened one mile away at a location on Hawthorne Avenue before closing just a few years later. (Courtesy of Rob Saye.)

Widespread Panic played a free concert in downtown Athens on April 18, 1998—the show is still regarded as one of the largest album release parties in music history. (Courtesy of Terry Allen.)

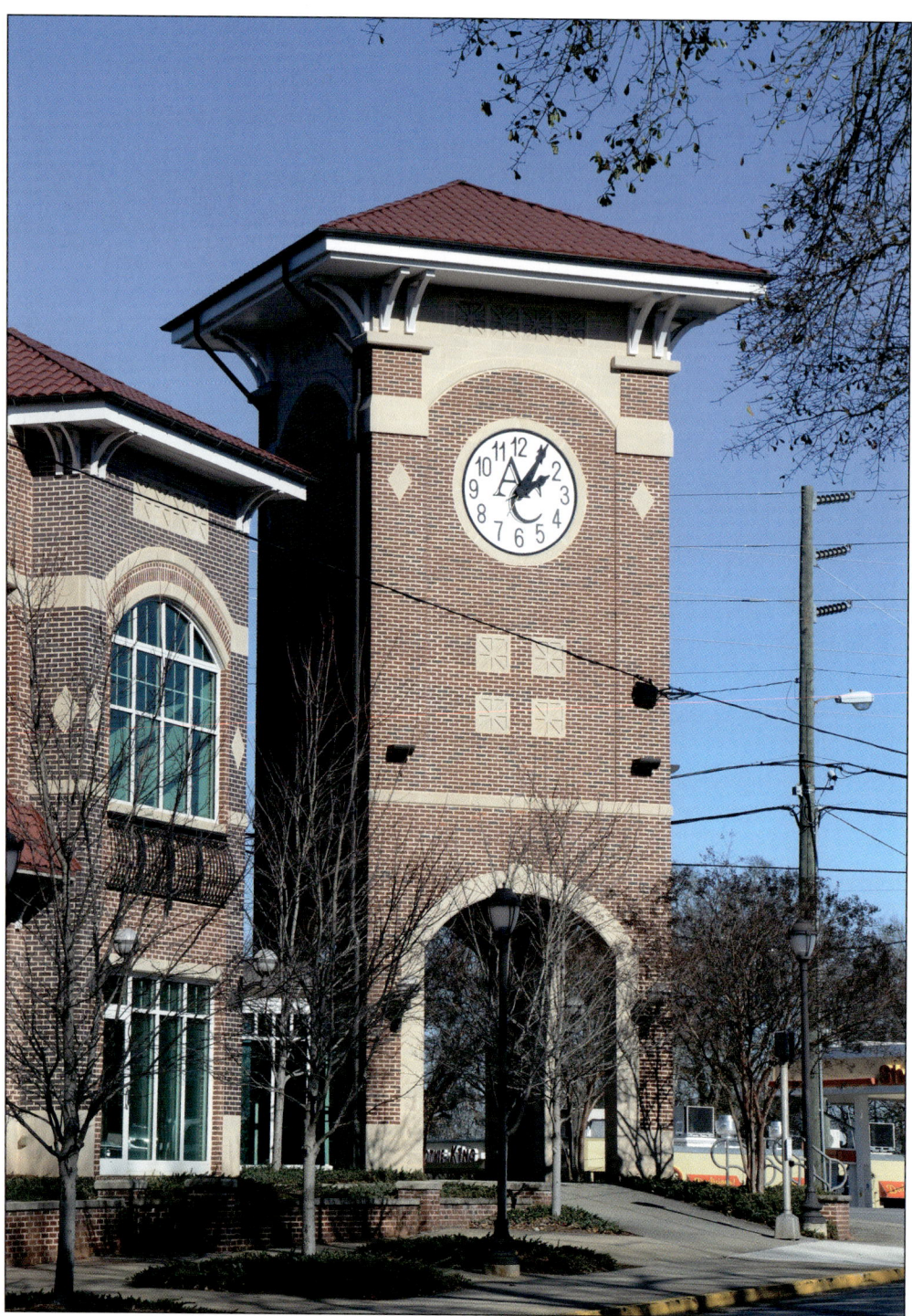

Construction was completed in 2004 on Fire Station No. 3 and the Five Points clock tower, located at Five Points (where Milledge Avenue and Lumpkin Street meet). This was formerly the location of the old Downtowner Inn. The clock's face displays a large "AC" for the unified government of Athens-Clarke County. (Courtesy of McGinnis Leathers.)

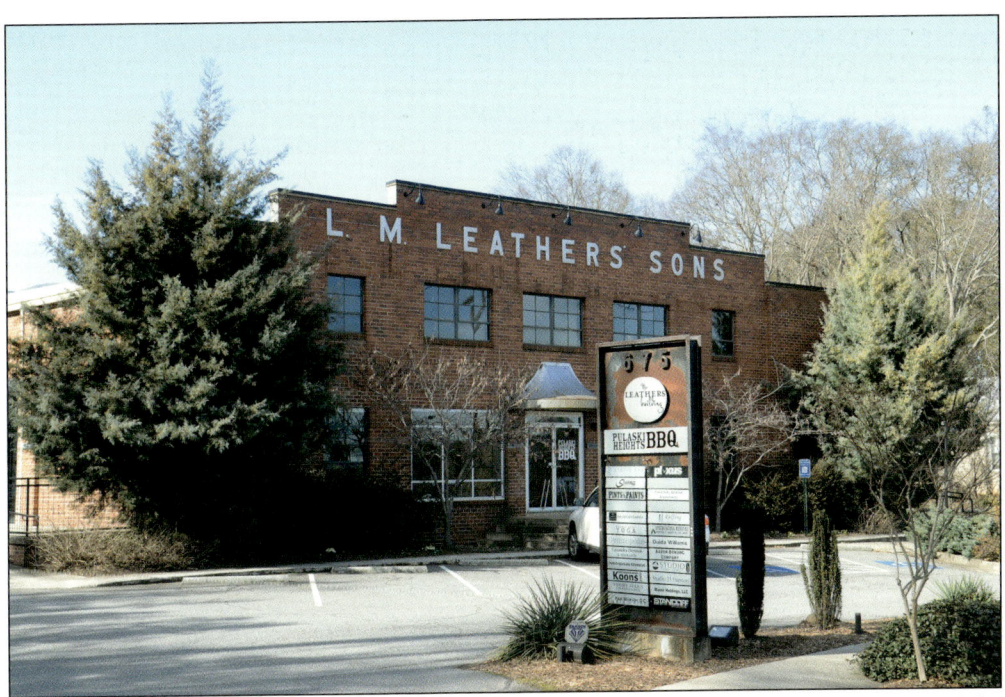

From 1946 to the 1990s, the L.M. Leathers' Sons manufacturing company operated out of the Leathers Building on Pulaski Street before moving into a newer, nicer facility. In 2005, the Leathers family negotiated the sale of its building to a developer who kept the name and historic appearance of the building intact. (Courtesy of McGinnis Leathers.)

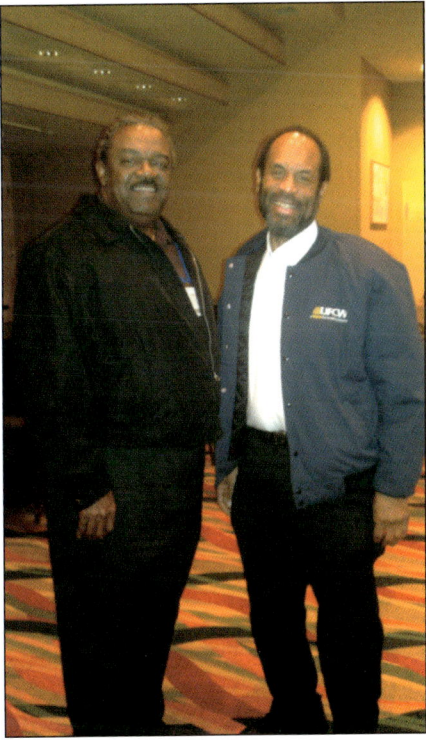

Pictured in 2012, friends Frank Platt (left) and James "Jimmy" Hurley originally met in Atlanta, but both became prominent African American figures in Athens. Platt was one of the city's first black policemen and served as chief of police for the Clarke County School District from 1998 until his retirement in 2011. As a member of the 1967 Bullpups freshman team, Hurley was the first black football player at UGA. (Courtesy of Frank Platt.)

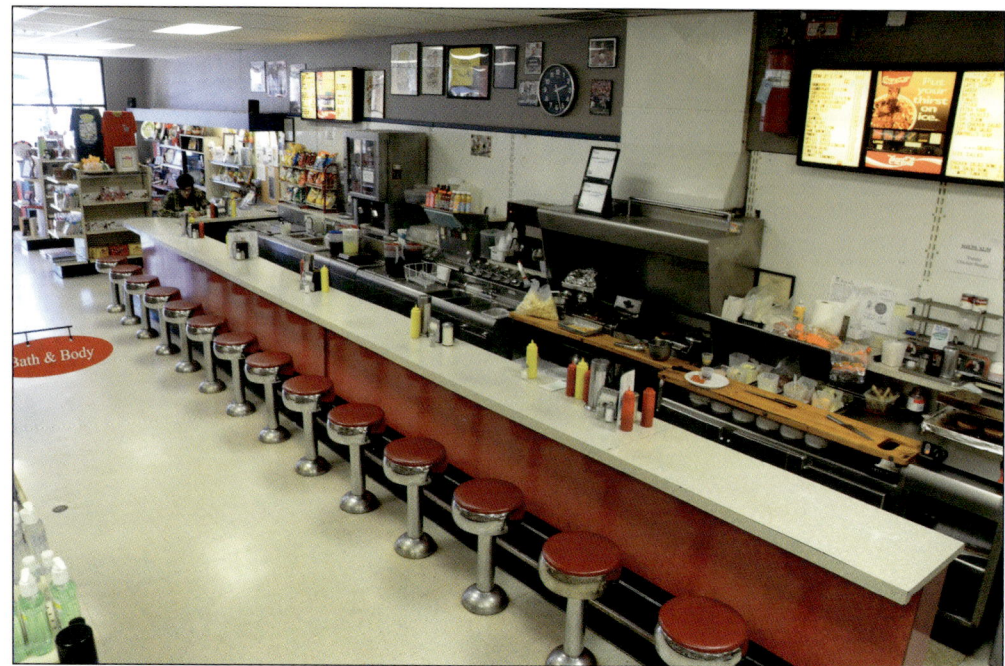

Known for its eclectic gifts and the delicious food it serves at its old-fashioned lunch counter, Add Drug Store has been a "one stop shop for the Five Points area" for decades. In 2011, the drugstore celebrated its 50th anniversary and was voted "Best Pharmacy" in the Online Athens Reader's Choice Awards a year later. (Courtesy of McGinnis Leathers.)

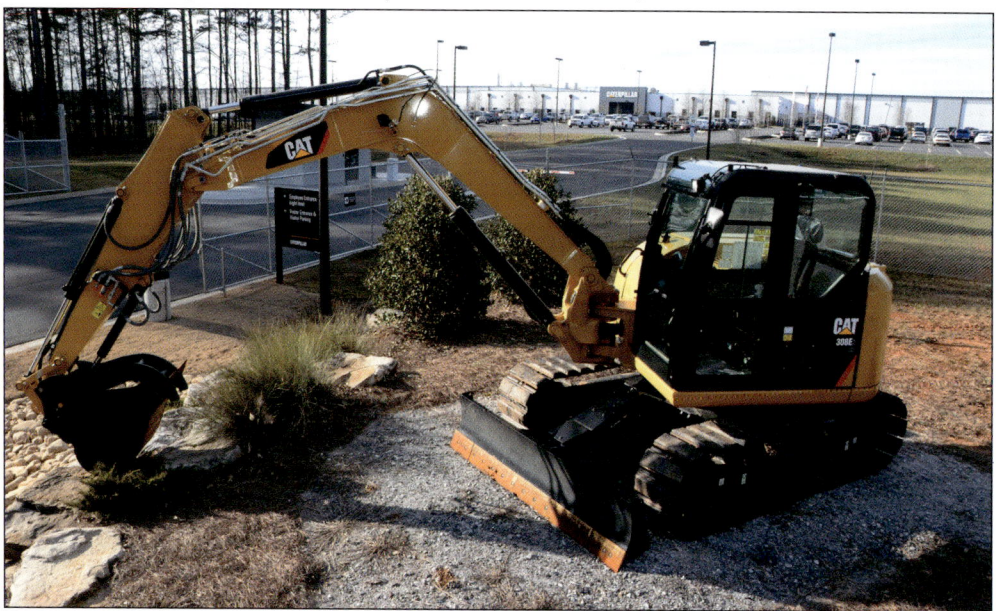

After much anticipation, Caterpillar celebrated the grand opening for its new Athens manufacturing plant on October 31, 2013. The state-of-the-art, 850,000-square-foot facility initially produced small track-type tractors and mini hydraulic excavators while employing over 1,000 people. The plant is actually located in Bogart, just outside of Athens, on a 780-acre site. (Courtesy of McGinnis Leathers.)

Two

STUDENT AND CAMPUS LIFE

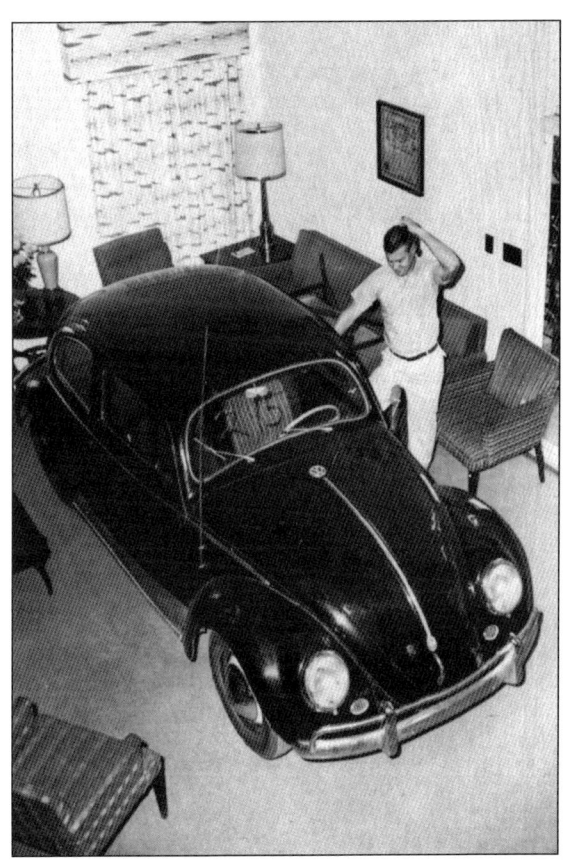

In the early 1960s, as school enrollment surpassed 10,000 students, the men's housing situation on campus became "critical" with overcrowding, as depicted in this photograph. More than 1,000 male students were forced to live off campus, with three men to two-man dorm rooms or even residing in what had been television lounging areas and dining rooms.

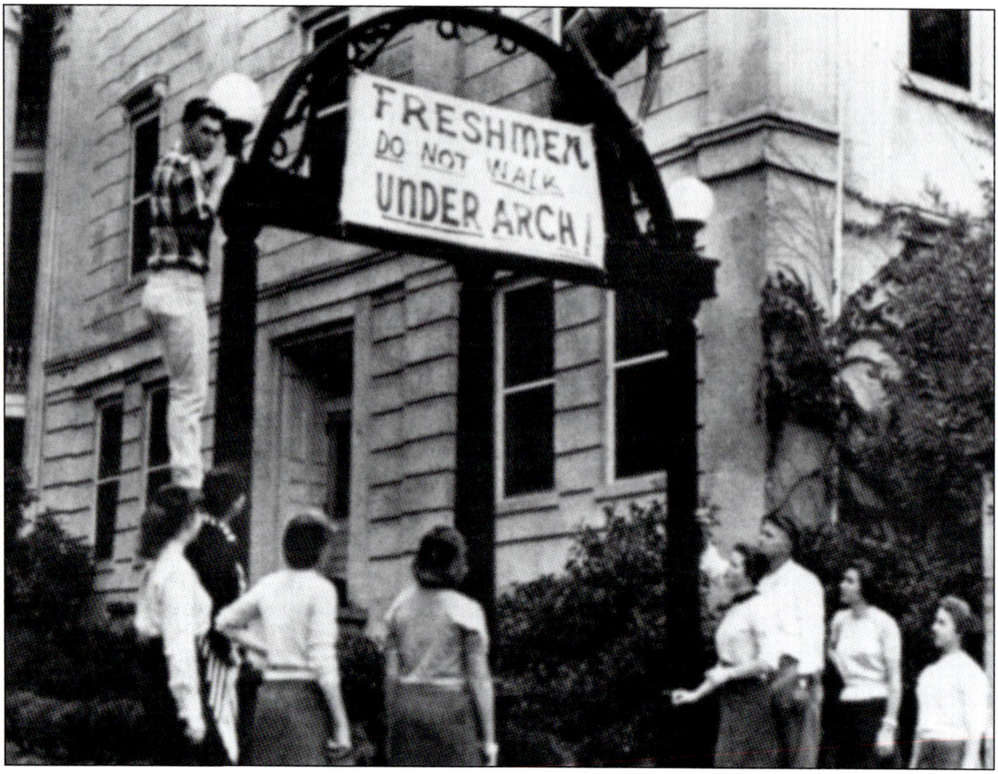

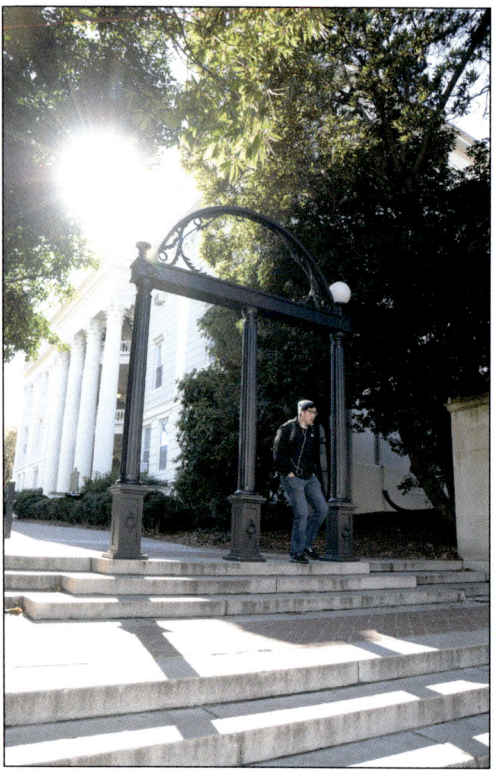

A cast-iron representation of the Georgia state seal, The Arch is a long-standing landmark of the University of Georgia. A legend that reportedly originated in 1909 or 1910 states that if a student walks under the Arch during his or her freshmen year, he or she will be destined for failure and will not graduate from UGA. As shown in the 1961 image above, the legend was still observed more than 50 years later; a plea in the student newspaper, *The Red and Black*, read, "Respect [the Arch's] tradition, freshmen. Don't walk between its pillars yet!" In the 2010s, the "no freshmen" sign might be gone, but the legend persists. (At left, courtesy of McGinnis Leathers.)

On January 9, 1961, it was reported that "two Negro students [Charlayne A. Hunter, 18, and Hamilton Holmes, 19], apparently destined to become the first of their race to attend the previously all-white University of Georgia, arrived on campus this morning to be met by a fleet of newsmen and photographers representing papers and magazines across the nation." In the following year's *Pandora*, UGA's yearbook, Hunter's photograph is included amongst other juniors.

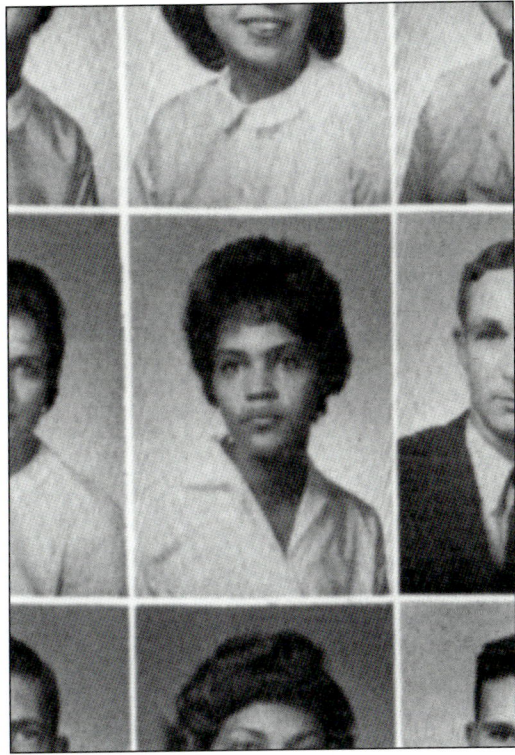

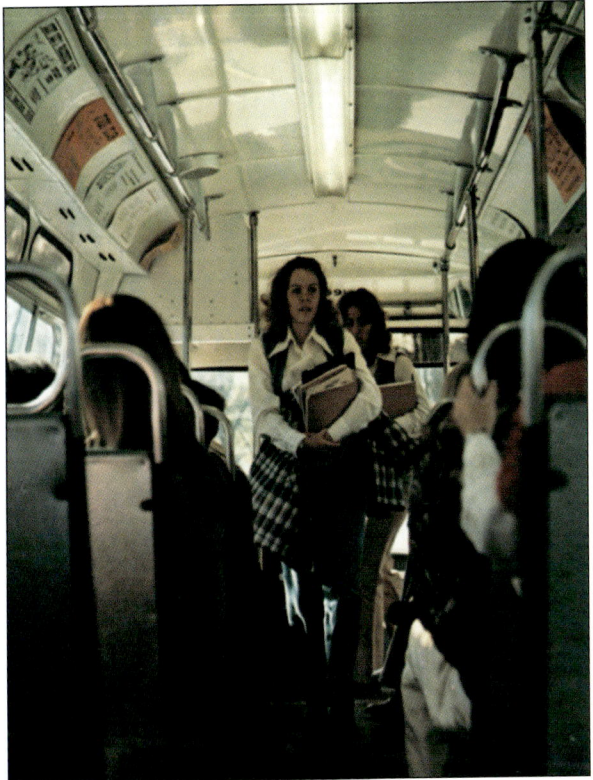

UGA implemented its intra-campus bus system on an experimental basis in the spring of 1967, operating it at full capacity—two routes and five total buses, with a fare of 5¢ per trip—by the winter of 1968. By that time, it was estimated that the buses' student load had increased tenfold since the fall of 1967.

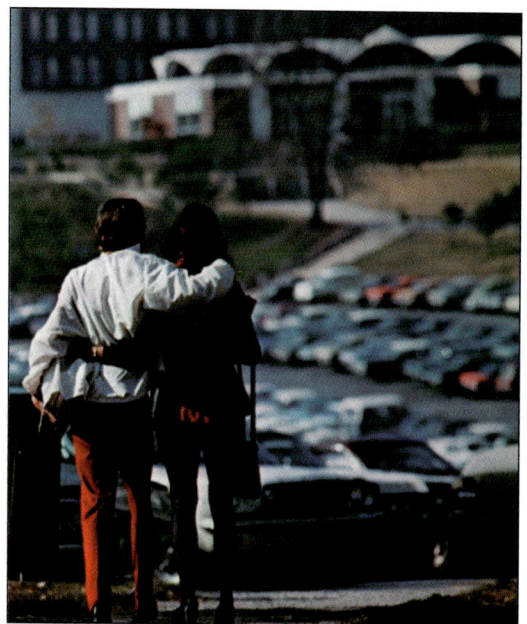

This unidentified student couple appears to be searching a parking lot for their car in the late 1960s. In 1969, UGA was presented with the problem of too many automobiles on campus and not enough parking spaces to accommodate them. In the fall of that year, there were approximately 8,000 automobiles registered to students, yet until October, the only parking spaces issued to them were in a lot near the Georgia Coliseum and an area behind Russell Hall, a student dormitory.

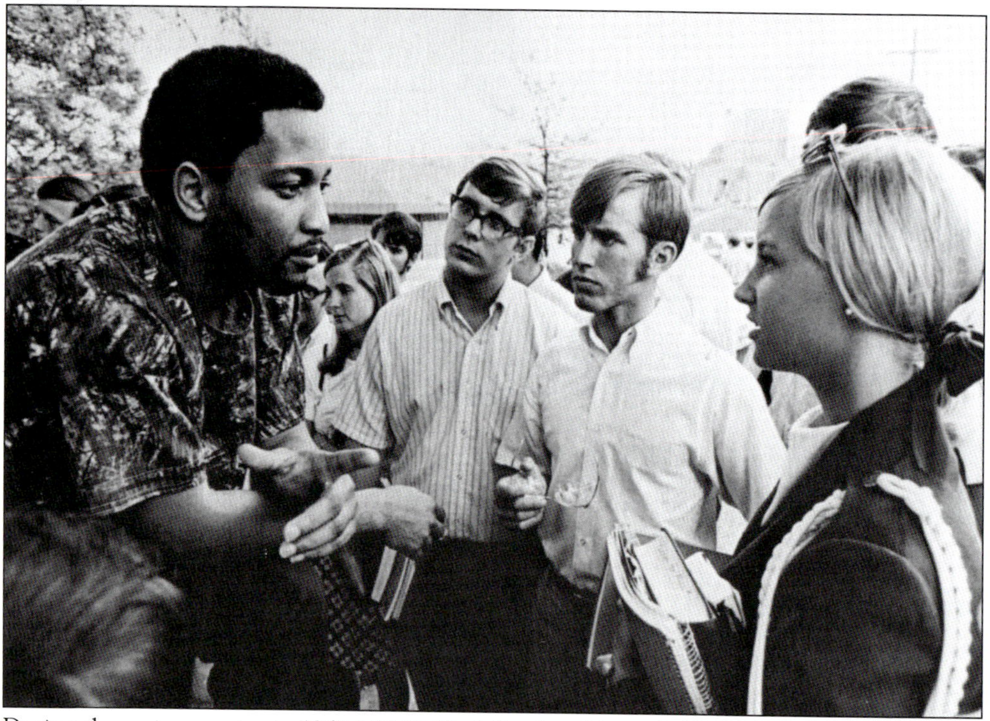

During the spring quarter in 1969, UGA's Black Student Union held a number of rallies like the one seen here. The BSU also presented the school administration with a list of more than 20 demands "for changes and innovations" in dealing with African American students, including "the active recruitment of black scholars and athletes," "the immediate cessation of the playing of 'Dixie' at University functions," that "Kappa Alpha [a traditional Southern men's social fraternity] be banned from campus," and that "a fund be established to aid black students who are suffering financial difficulty."

On October 15, 1969, "Vietnam Moratorium" demonstrations took place across the nation, including in Athens. The Athens program was held on the UGA campus and drew what was described as a "massive audience," including this young girl wearing a sign that declares, "War is not healthy for children and other living things."

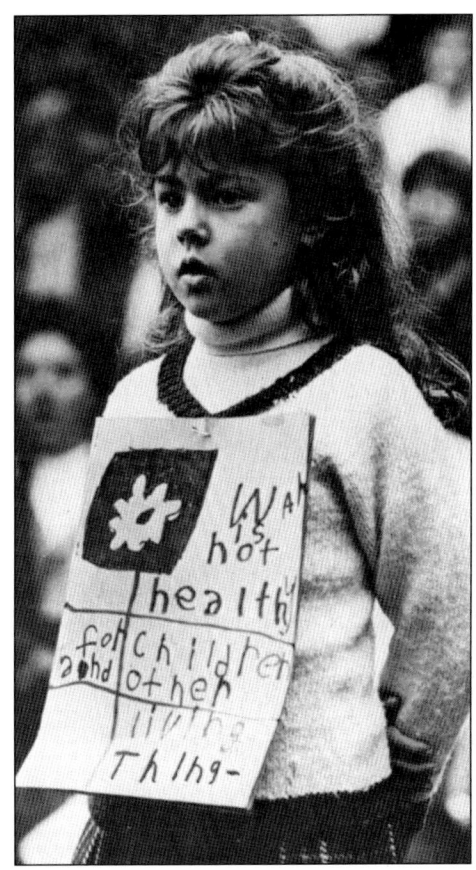

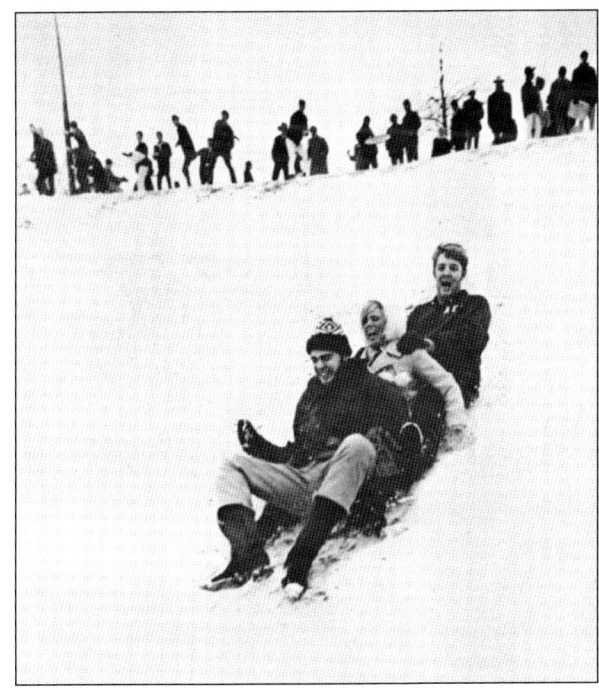

UGA students enjoyed the massive snowstorm that hit Athens in January 1970, dropping the temperature in the city to around zero degrees Fahrenheit for several consecutive days. It got so cold that the section of the Oconee River running through downtown Athens froze to a point at which people could literally walk on the water.

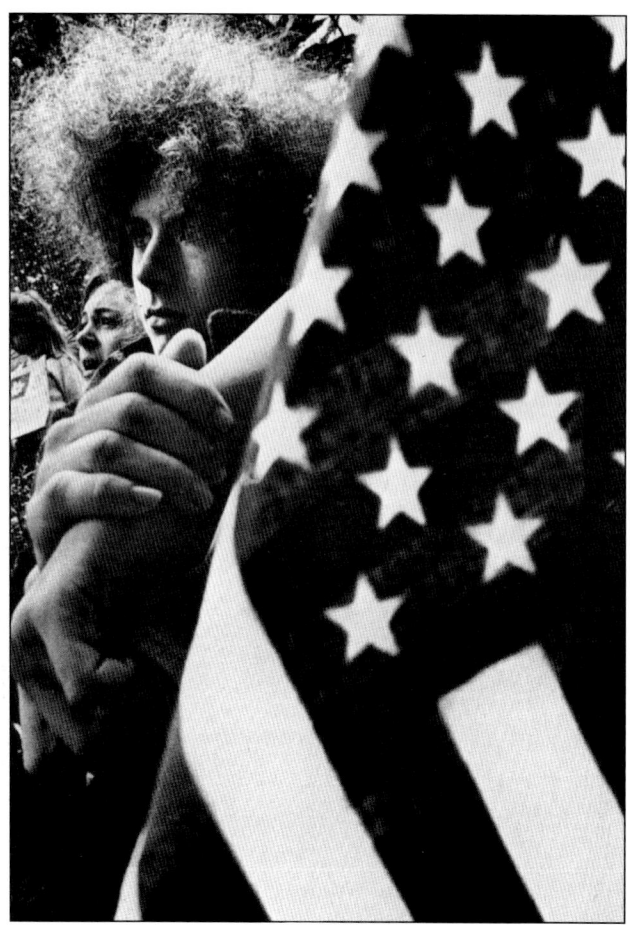

In April 1970, during a protest against UGA's complicity with the Vietnam War, specifically the ROTC's presence on campus, 30 to 40 protestors entered a UGA military building. In the end, there was no violence during the demonstration, just a tense moment when a protestor removed the US flag from the military building. A student promptly replaced the seized flag, which was again removed but then replaced for a second time.

One of the largest demonstrations ever held at a higher institution of learning in the state of Georgia occurred on the UGA campus in May 1970 in protest of the murders of four Kent State University students who were killed while demonstrating against Pres. Richard Nixon's decision to send US troops into Cambodia during the Vietnam War. Although a number of rocks were thrown, breaking glass during the protest, most of the estimated 4,000 demonstrators were nonviolent.

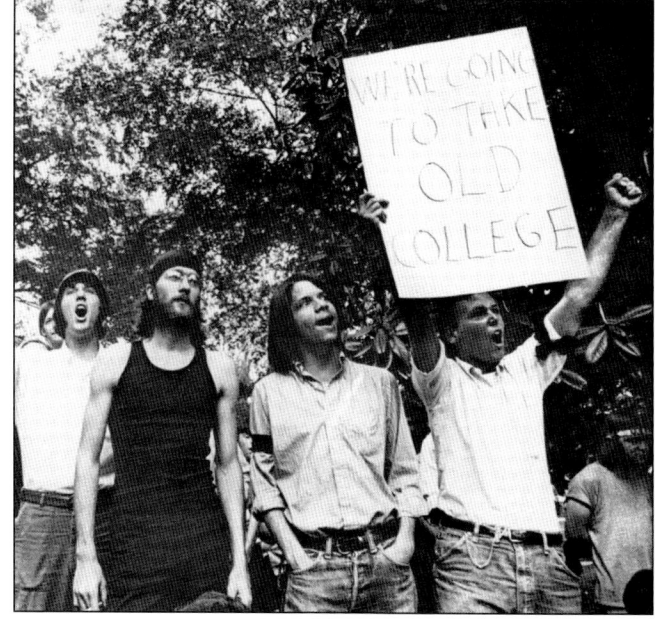

In the early 1970s, the UGA student population was characterized as open to religion and tolerant toward different religious groups. There was actually student demand for more religion courses to be taught at the school. According to a UGA student in 1971, "A year ago if I wanted to talk about religion I would have to bring up the subject myself. Now people reach out to me!"

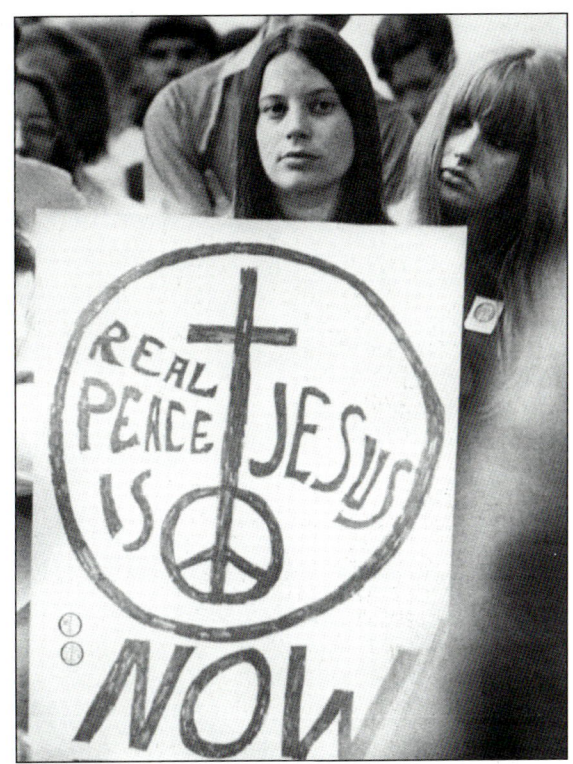

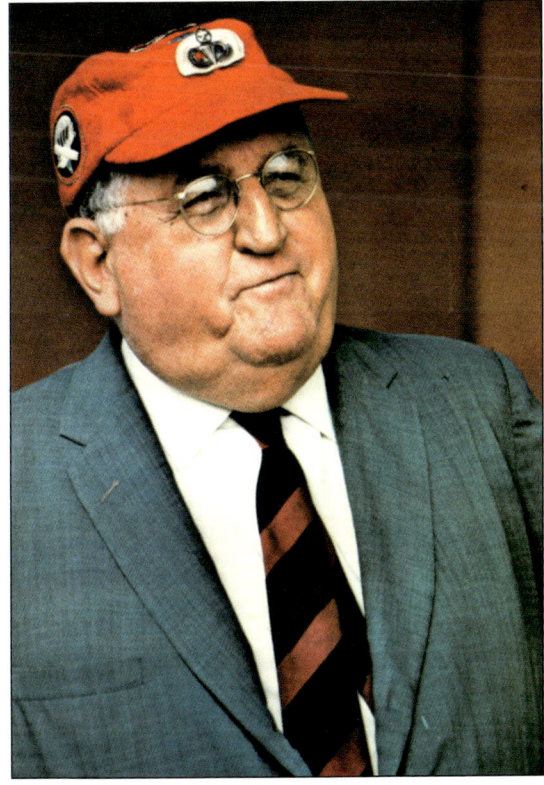

William Tate is pictured here in 1971, his final year as dean of men at UGA after serving in the position since 1946. Tate, a UGA graduate, was affiliated with the university in some form for most of his life. In his service as a communication bridge between the school's administration and its students, Tate is still considered possibly the most popular staff member in the school's history. He passed away in 1980 on his 77th birthday.

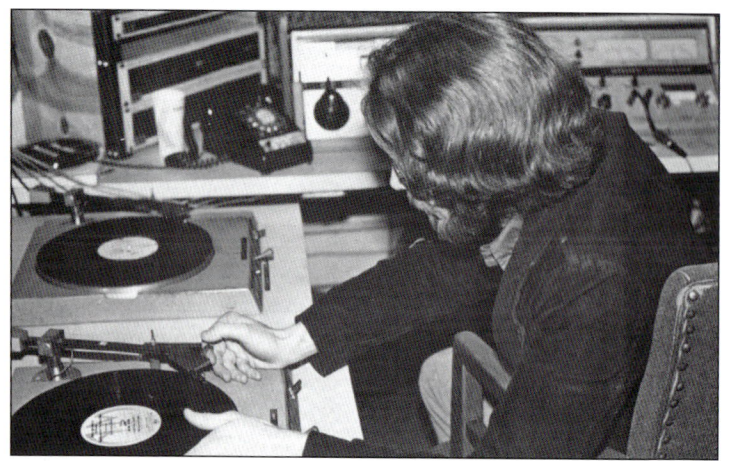

UGA's campus radio station, WUOG 90.5, celebrated its 40th anniversary in 2012. The station, which was launched on October 16, 1972, initially had a broadcast range of 35 to 40 miles and played contemporary, top 40 music "without bubblegum" from 6:30 a.m. to 5:00 p.m., Monday through Friday.

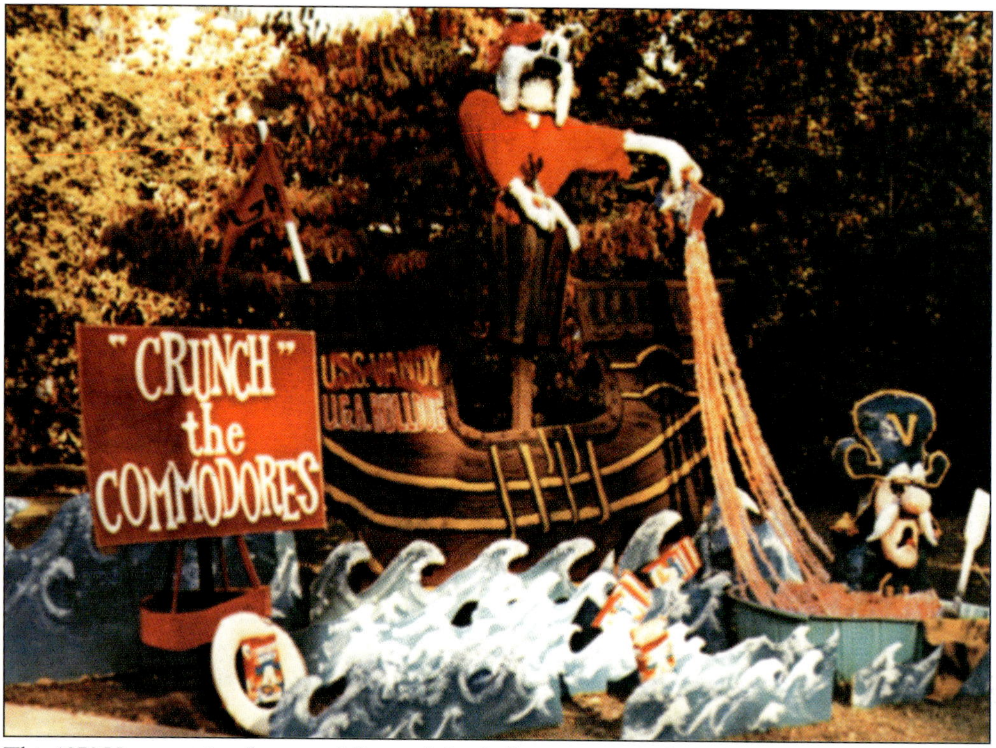

This 1972 Homecoming float urged Georgia's football team to "crunch the [Vanderbilt] Commodores," which the Bulldogs did by a score of 28-3; however, the big news during that particular Homecoming week was a male student's attempt at becoming UGA's Homecoming queen. Randy Ascher, a graduate student in political science, said his main purpose in running was to make the selection process "more humanistic and less subjective" than it had been in the past. In the end, Ascher did not win and was not even selected amongst five finalists.

At a time when streaking nude was a nationwide phenomenon, 1,543 UGA students ran naked across the Sanford Stadium bridge on March 7, 1974, to set the world record for the largest group streak. Apparently, the large number of streakers multiplied after a streaking episode a few days before, during which Athens police threw tear gas to disperse a large crowd that had congregated after the arrest of a single male streaker.

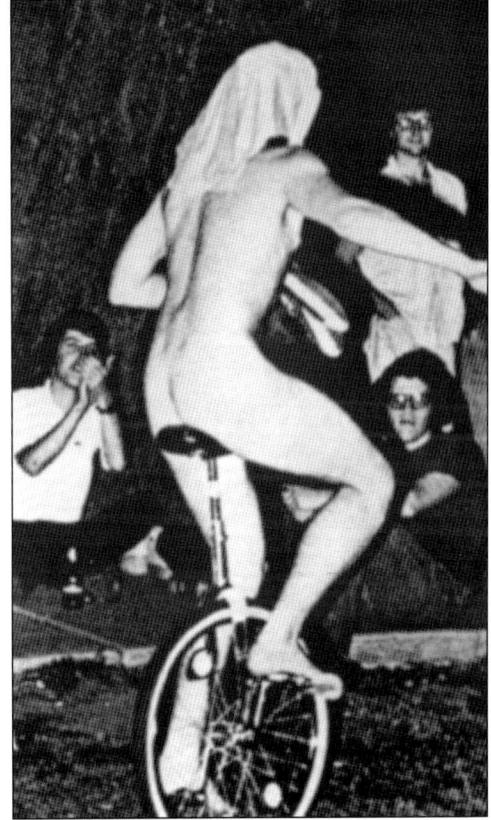

This image shows a UGA sociology professor instructing a class during the 1973–1974 academic year. Of the 20,318 students enrolled at the university that fall, 42.7 percent were female, an increase from the year before, while 2.6 percent were African American, a slight decrease. Forty years later, in 2013, the first-year students entering UGA were 60 percent female and 8.4 percent African American.

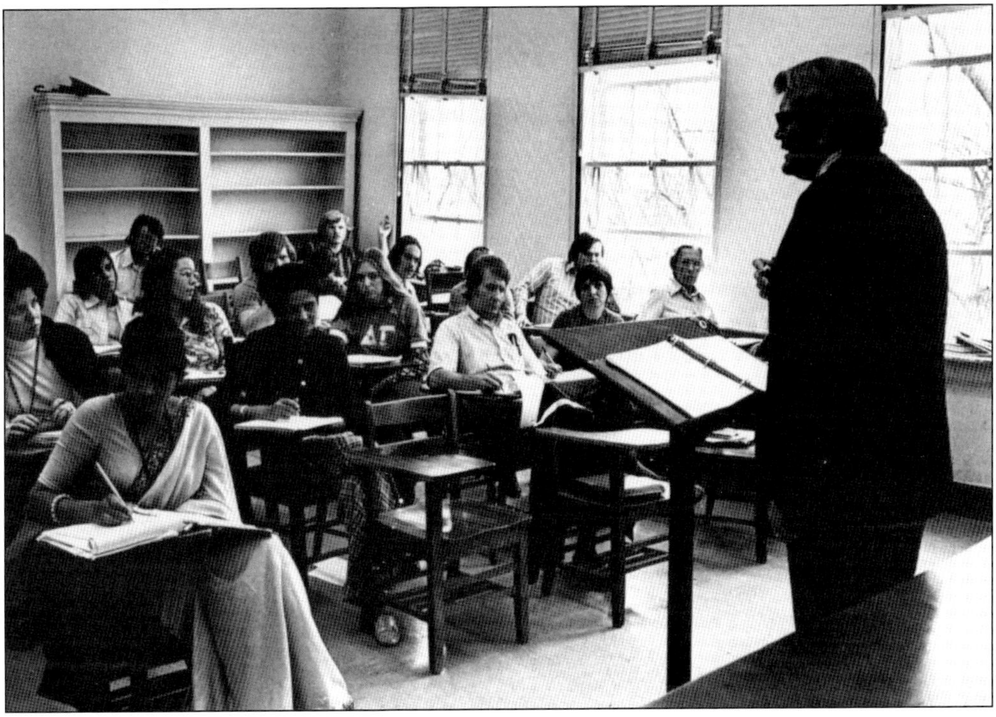

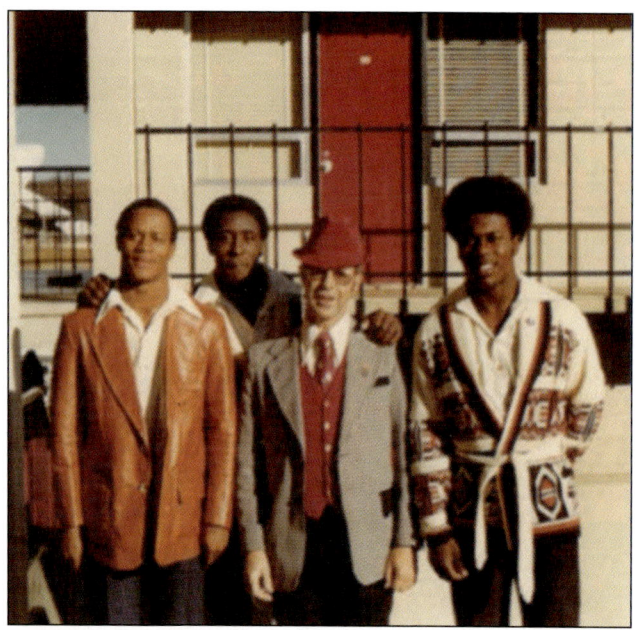

This 1976 image shows, from left to right, UGA cornerback Robert Hope, linebacker Ricky McBride, head trainer Warren Morris, and running back Willie McClendon in front of McWhorter Hall. McWhorter Hall, built in 1967, primarily served as the "athlete's dorm" before it was demolished in 2005, nearly 40 years after it opened. (Courtesy of D.J. Pascale.)

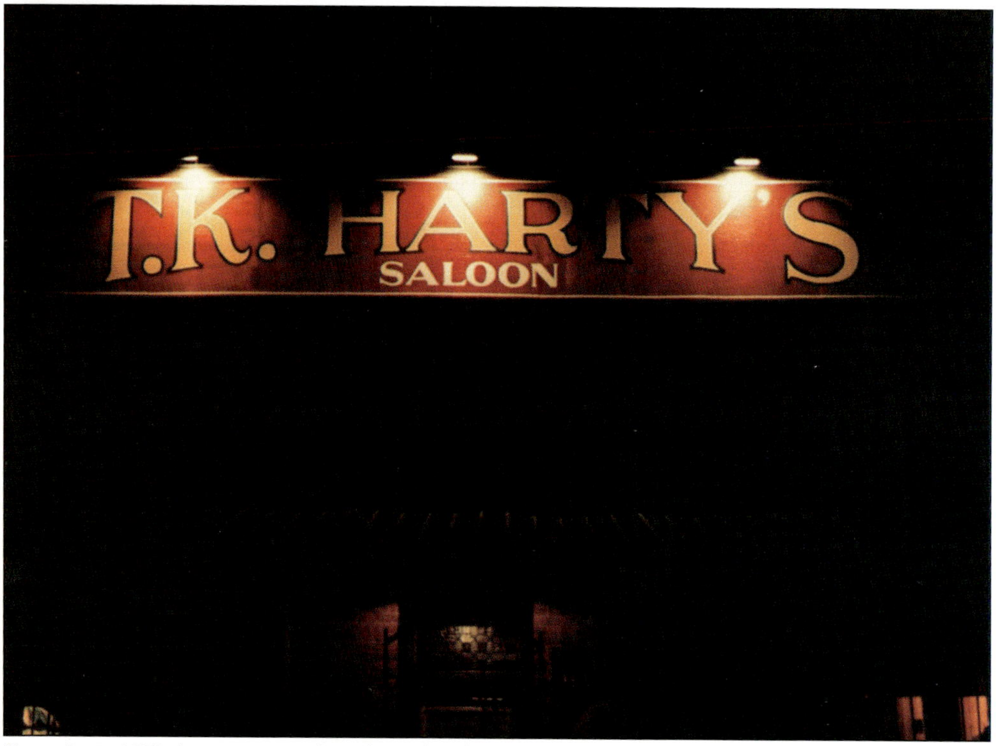

From June 1972 (just in time for when the drinking age in Georgia dropped from 21 to 18 on July 1 of that year) through 1990, T.K. Harty's Saloon, located at The Station on Hoyt Street, was a favorite drinking establishment amongst UGA students. The saloon, originally owned by Theodore K. Harty and Frank Range, initially offered students a number of things most local bars did not: pizza, sandwiches, cleanliness, and an outside deck. In 1977, Harty was murdered by a hit man hired by the owner of a rival pizza restaurant.

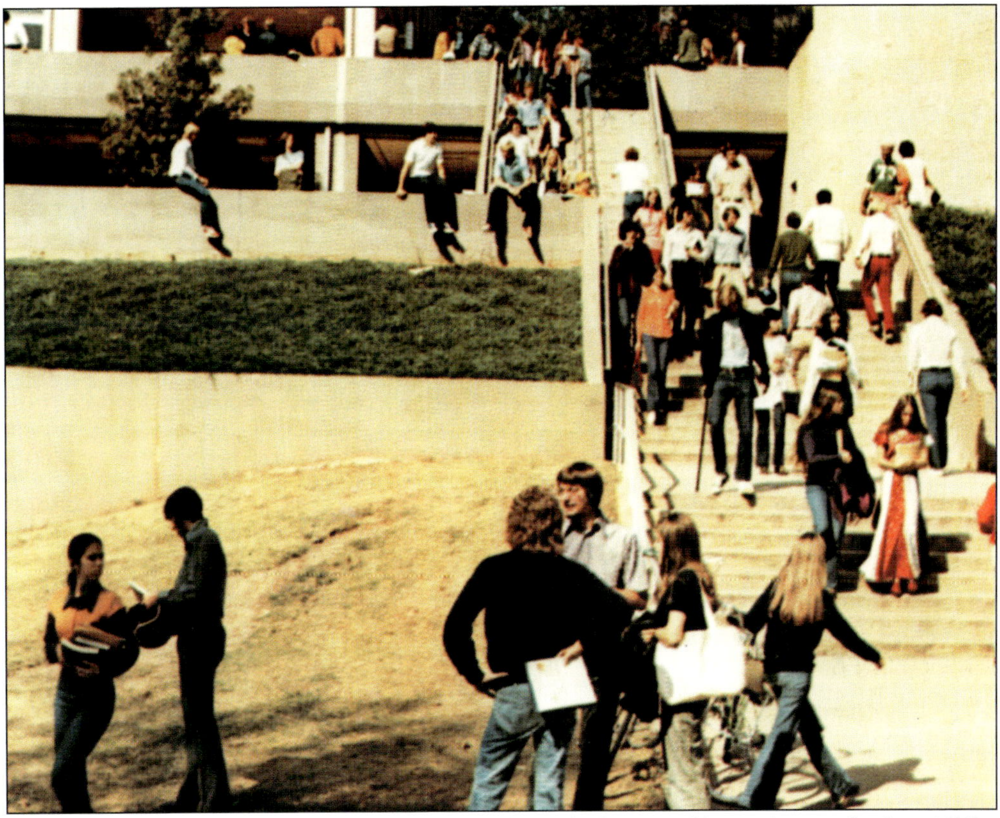

This photograph shows UGA's Journalism and Psychology Buildings during the late 1970s, including the location's multiple sets of stairs. Athens, which means "city of hills" in Greek, is a rather hilly city and thus appropriately named; UGA has been recognized as containing more on-campus stairs than most colleges.

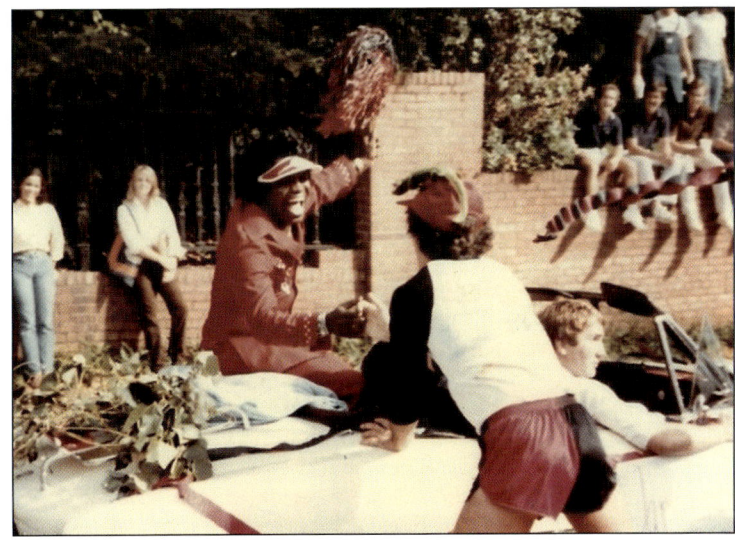

James Brown, the "Godfather of Soul," was twice an integral part of UGA's Homecoming: in 1981 as a special guest and in 1995 as the grand marshal. This image from the 1981 Homecoming parade shows Brown greeting an excited Georgia Bulldogs fan while cruising away from downtown on South Lumpkin Street. (Courtesy of Rob Saye.)

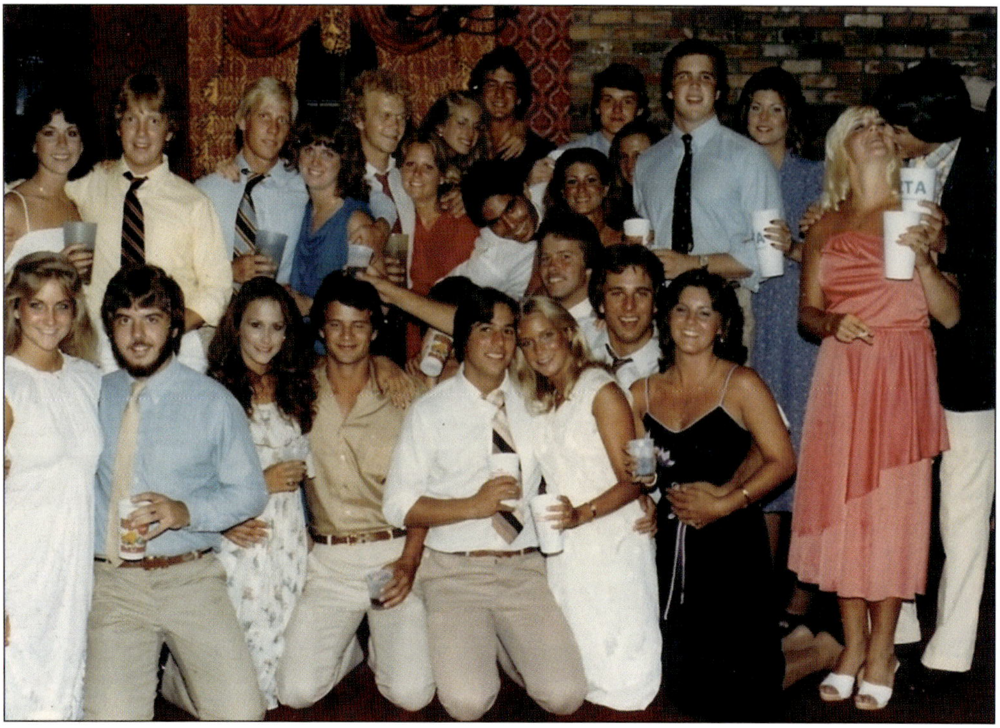

During the fall of 1980, around the time this Greek social occurred, Greeks at UGA were described in *The Red and Black*, the campus newspaper, as "fraternity and sorority members who wear khaki pants, Izod shirts, Docksider shoes, and 'blow dryer' hairstyles." The reporter also suggested that the Greeks may experience "some problems" that particular academic year since the state's new legal drinking age had been increased to 19 years of age. (Courtesy of Rob Saye.)

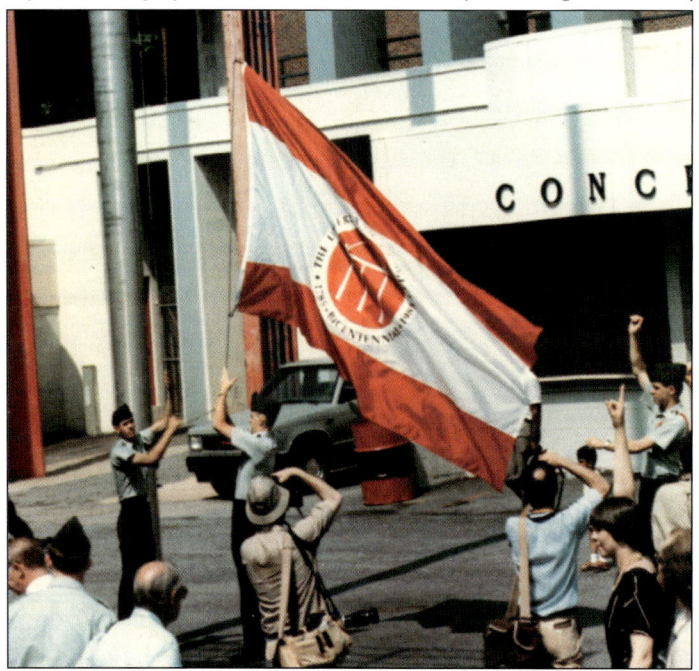

During the summer of 1984, students raised UGA's bicentennial flag to officially begin a 16-month celebration of the university's 200th birthday. Although the school was founded in 1785 as the first state-chartered university in the United States, classes did not actually begin at UGA until 1801.

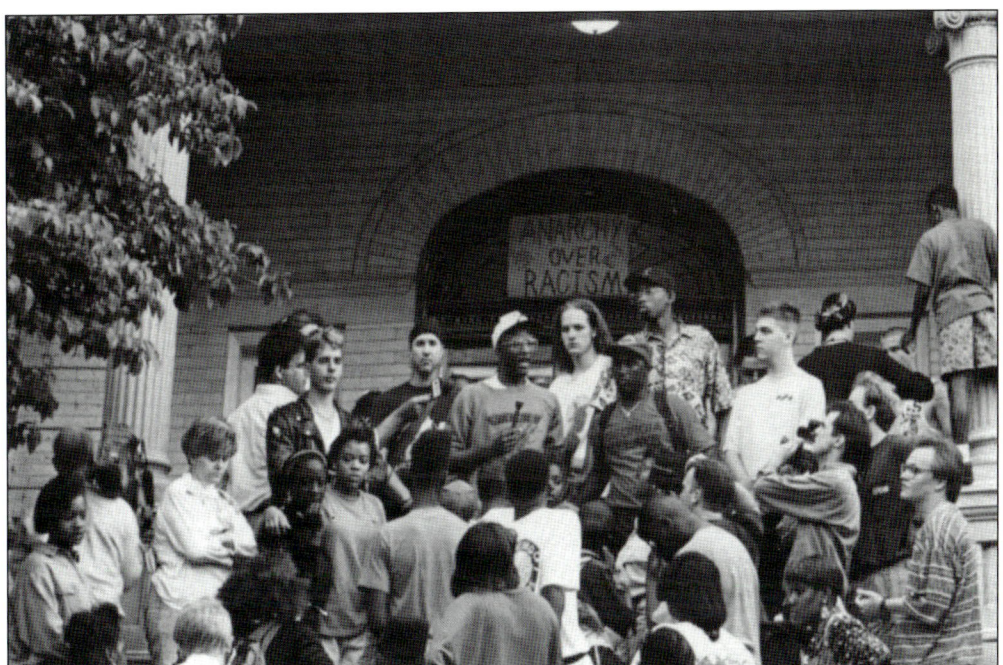

In response to the verdict in the Rodney King trial, in which four Los Angeles police officers were acquitted of charges of assault with a deadly weapon and use of excessive force, UGA students and Athens residents—both black and white—gathered on the steps of Athens City Hall in April 1992. Unlike the riots transpiring thousands of miles away in Los Angeles, the protest in Athens was rather peaceful.

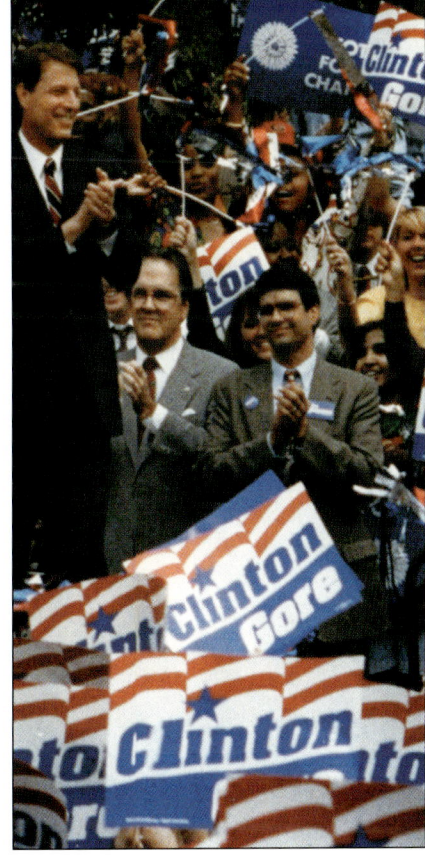

Encouraging students to "vote for a change," vice presidential candidate Al Gore spoke at the Tate Student Center Plaza on campus less than two weeks before the 1992 US presidential election.

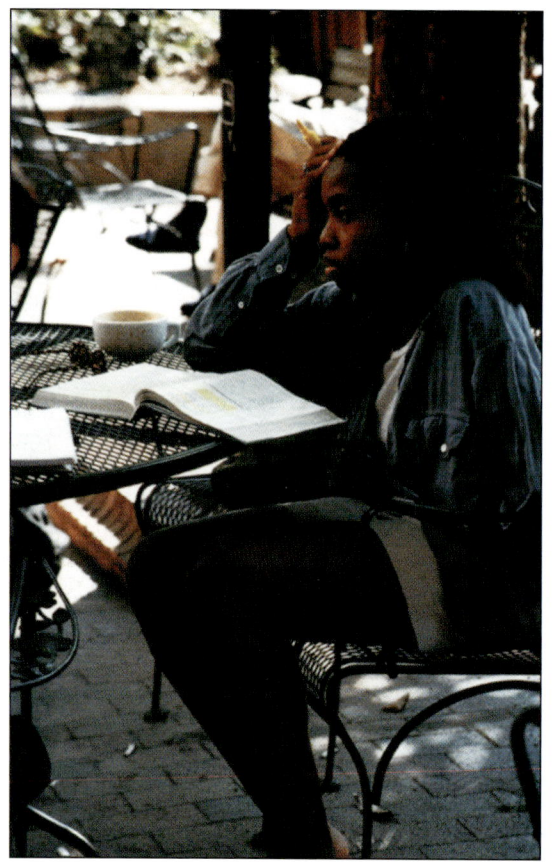

After a statewide lottery referendum was passed on November 3, 1992, Gov. Zell Miller's merit-based HOPE (Helping Outstanding Pupils Educationally) scholarship program went into effect. Originally, if a Georgia high school graduate qualified for the HOPE scholarship, he or she would be eligible to receive funds to finance their first year of tuition. However, in order to receive funding for a second year, the student had to keep hitting the books, maintaining at least a 3.0 grade point average at the end of the first year in college.

Piedmont College, headquartered in Demorest, Georgia, opened an Athens location in this two-story building on Prince Avenue in 1996 with a total enrollment of roughly 300 students. By 2014, the school was still based on the same street, but had expanded, at a different location, into seven separate buildings. The original Piedmont College building currently houses the Sparrow's Nest, a Christian ministry center. (Courtesy of McGinnis Leathers.)

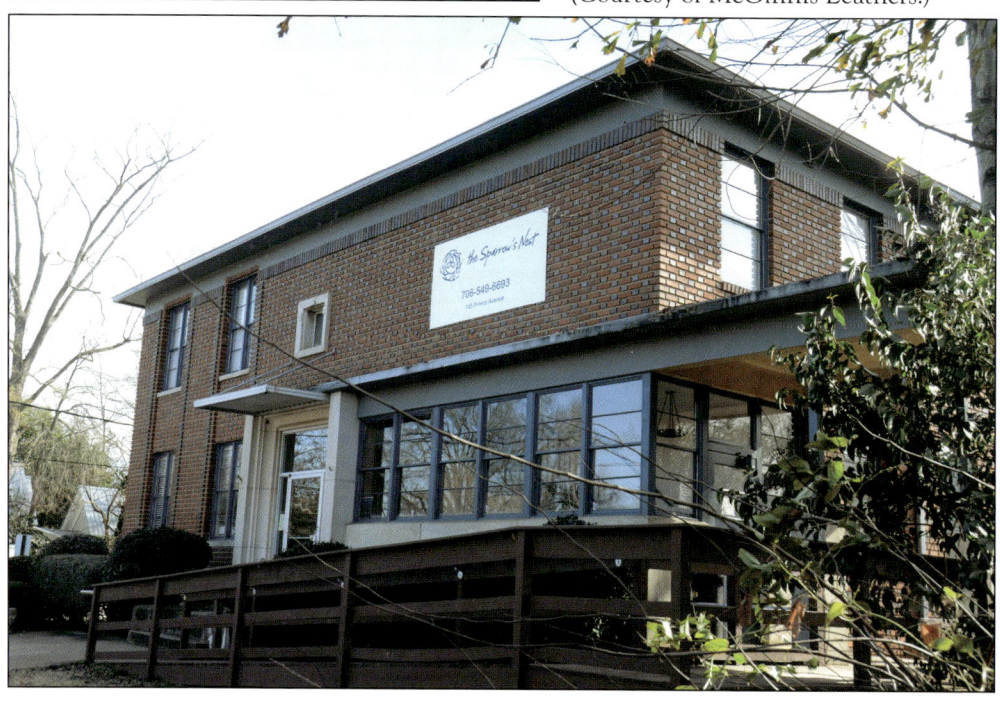

After the 1996 Summer Olympic Games, UGA began 21 construction projects on campus at a total cost of roughly $200 million, including the $10.6 million University Health Center. The facility opened its doors in January 1998 on East Campus and was originally one and a half times the size of the old Gilbert Health Center, which was located on North Campus.

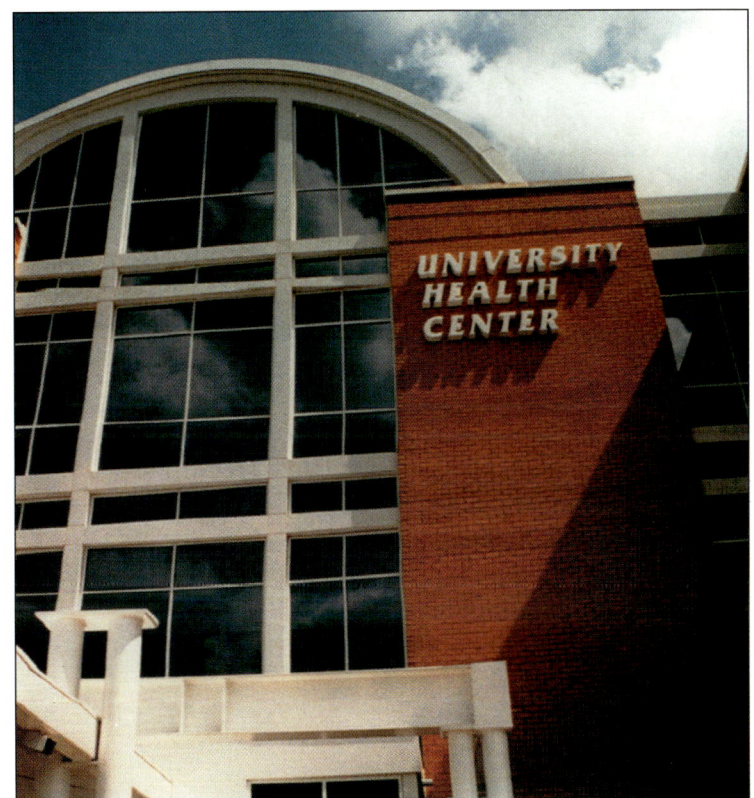

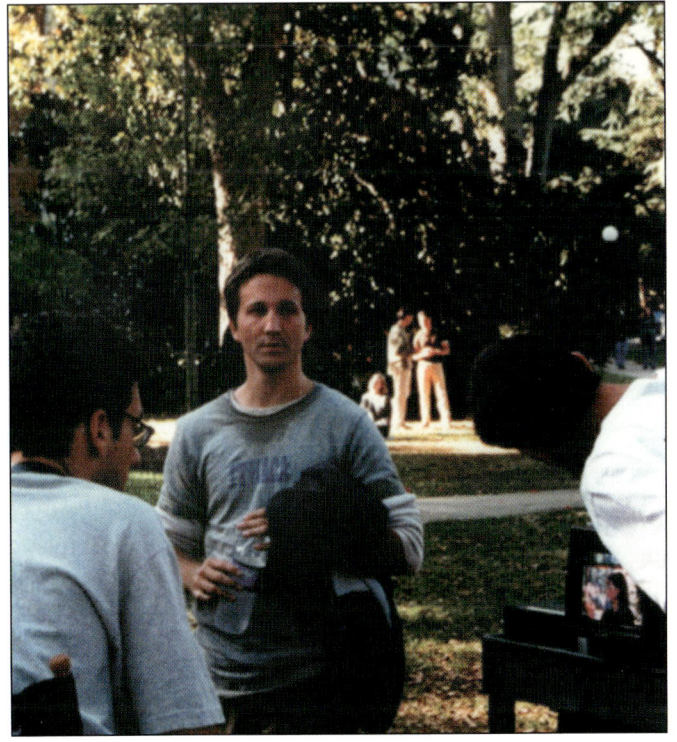

In this image from 1999, actor Breckin Meyer takes a break from filming the movie *Road Trip* on UGA's North Campus. For almost an entire week that October, scenes for the DreamWorks movie were filmed at several campus locations and used UGA students as non-speaking extras. Meyer said that filming in Athens was "like *Willy Wonka and the Chocolate Factory*, but with college kids."

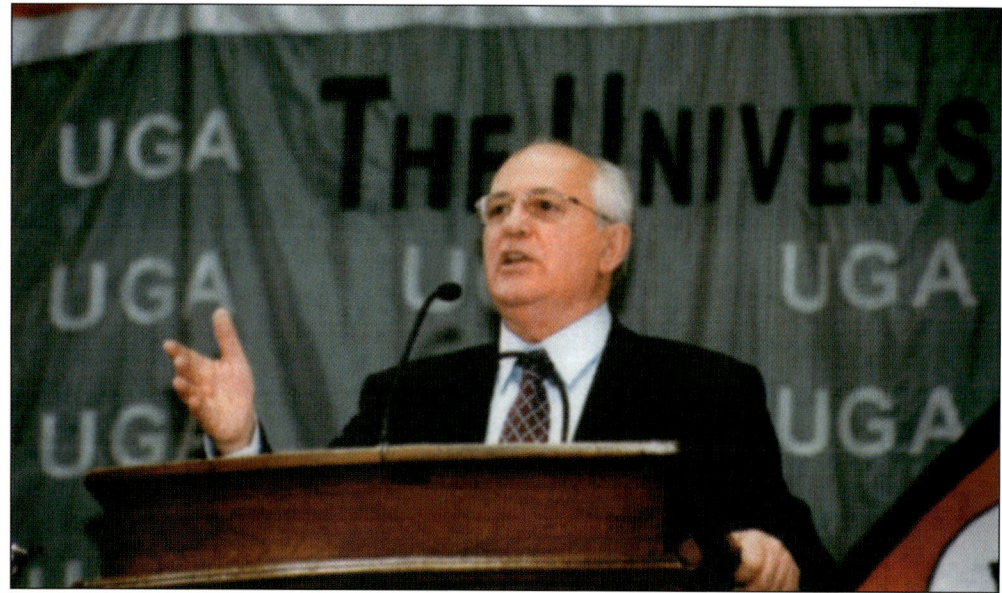

On December 3, 1999, Mikhail Gorbachev, who was once the most powerful man in the Communist world, spoke before a crowd of 11,500 at Stegeman Coliseum. While speaking about environmental issues and globalization, the distinguished and controversial former president of the Soviet Union declared, "The environmental challenge is the number-one challenge of the 21st century."

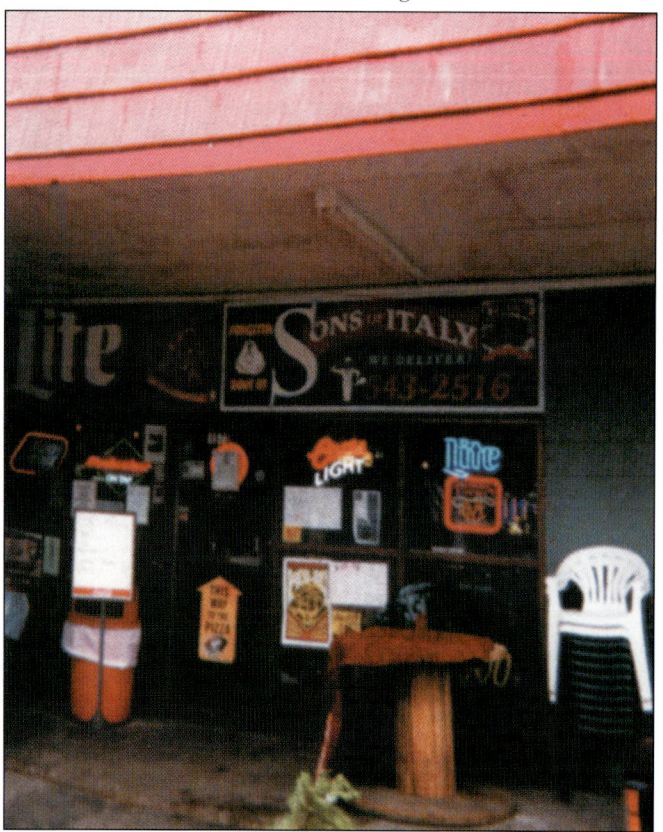

Sons of Italy, or simply "Sons," is pictured at its original location around 2000. From the early 1970s until the summer of 2007, the pizzeria once considered perhaps the only place in town "where students can drink during the week and consider themselves 'outside,' " was located in Five Points before moving to the Milledge Plaza near the intersection of Milledge Avenue and the Macon Highway.

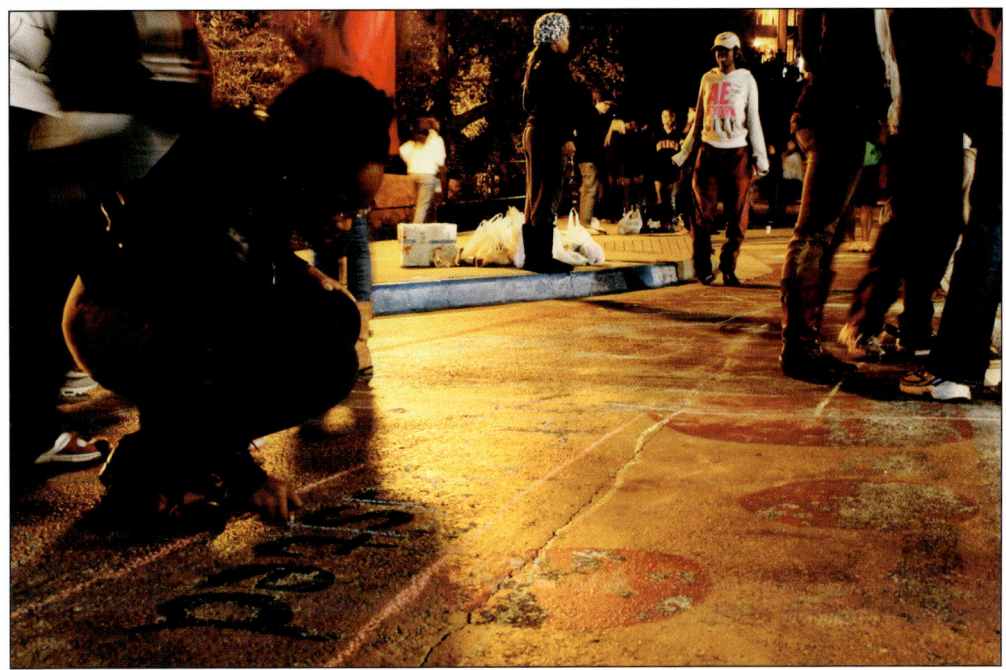

As demonstrated by an unidentified student in this photograph from October 2011, street painting on Sanford Drive is one of UGA's most popular traditions during the school's Homecoming week. Student groups routinely do their painting at night and early in the week.

Inspired by nationwide Occupy Wall Street demonstrations—protests over the greed and corruption in the financial sector—approximately 50 Athens residents and UGA students gathered at the Arch beginning on October 6, 2011. What was dubbed "Occupy Athens" began as a rally after New York City police arrested hundreds of Occupy Wall Street protesters the week before.

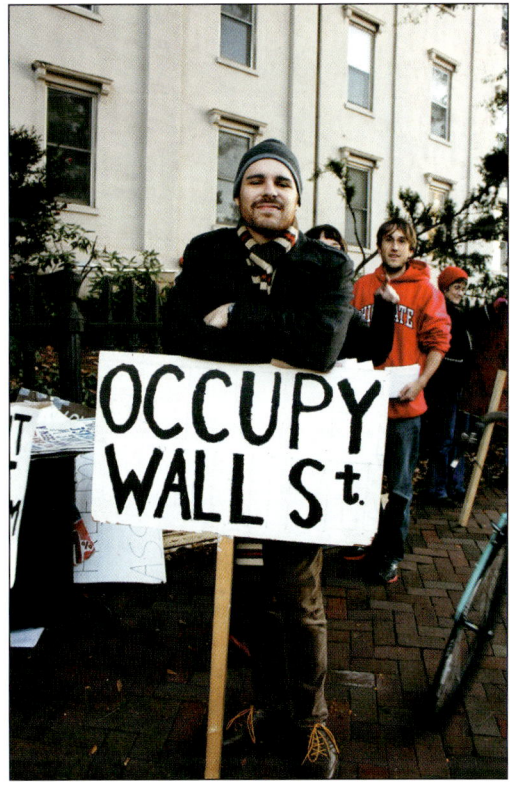

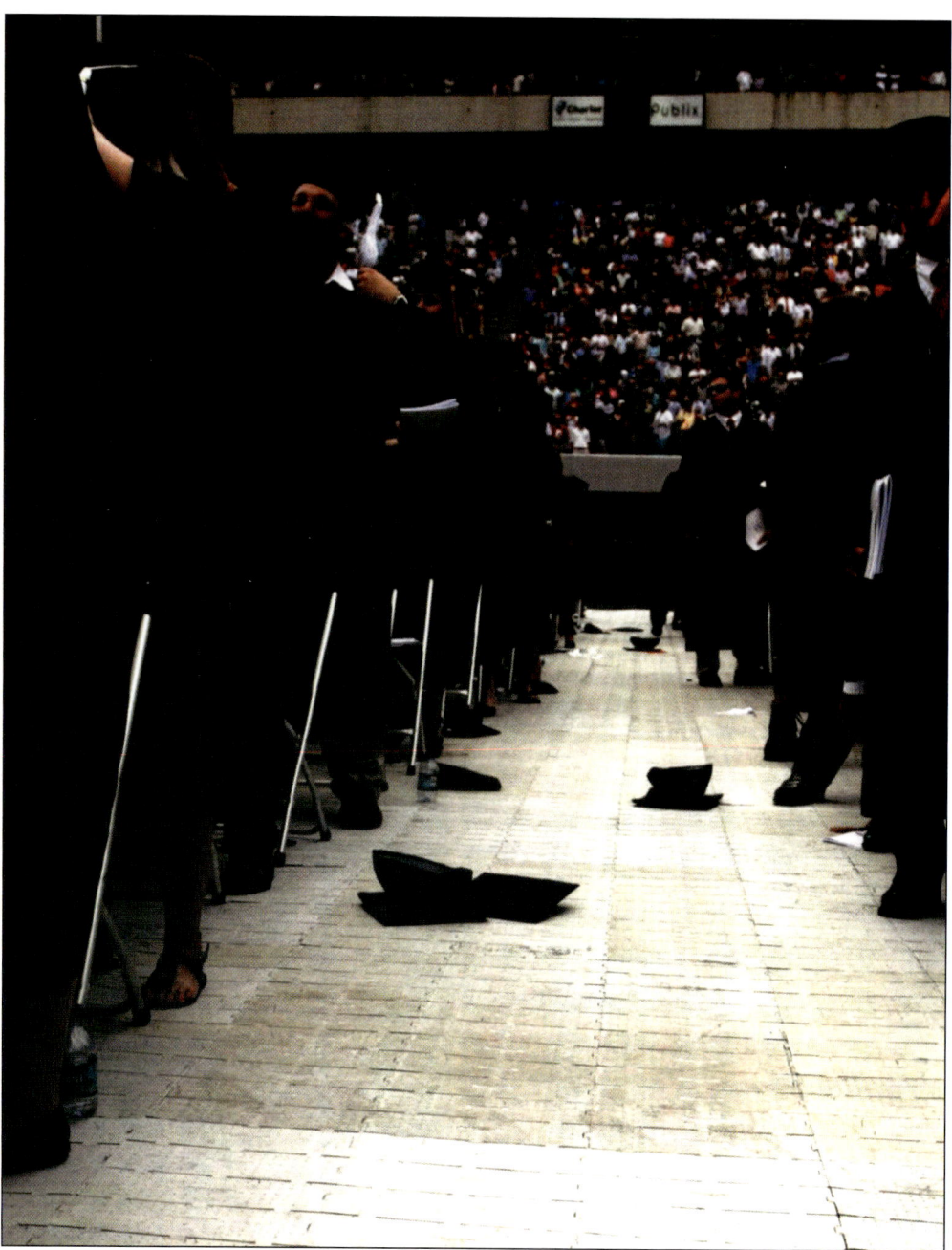

Starting in 1949, UGA began holding its spring commencement in Sanford Stadium. To illustrate the growth of the university during the "modern" era, roughly 1,200 graduating students gathered for spring commencement in 1959; compare this to the spring of 2013 (pictured), when approximately 5,255 students graduated: 4,164 undergraduates and 1,091 graduate students. During the 2013 graduation, Mary Frances Early—the first African American to earn a degree from UGA—was bestowed with the 79th honorary doctoral degree in the school's history.

Three

HISTORIC DOWNTOWN

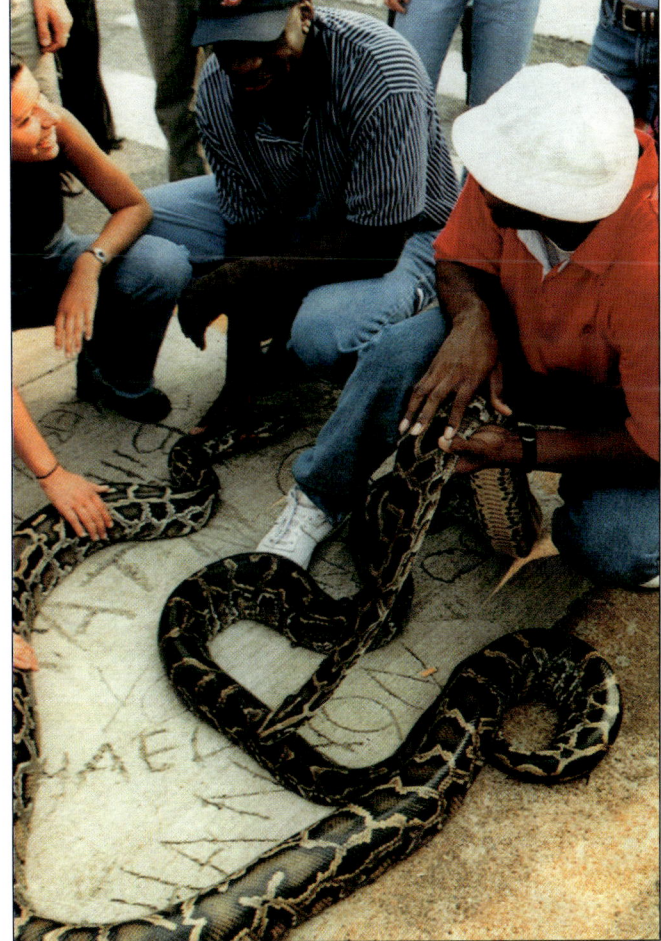

A person never knows whom, or what, they will encounter in the streets of downtown Athens, like these snakes pictured during the 1990s; however, the unpredictability of the downtown district has not necessarily always been present. Prior to the completion of the Georgia Square Mall in the early 1980s, downtown was primarily department and retail stores. Since then, the area has transitioned into a mixed-use district that offers a variety of stores, restaurants, entertainment, and residences.

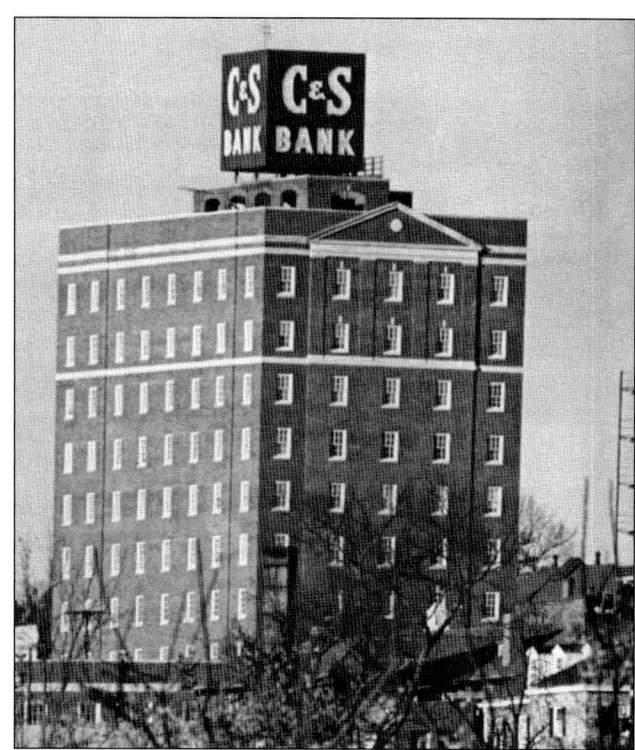

The downtown C&S building, pictured here in the early 1970s, featured one of Athens's most conspicuous landmarks: the big green C&S sign. In the early 1990s, NationsBank formed after acquiring C&S, and the Athens landmark had to be removed. Interestingly, the C&S sign was originally built to cover a rooftop cooling unit that had been installed on top of the former Holman Hotel.

This 1972 photograph, which looks left down East Clayton Street toward North Thomas Street during the holiday season, includes signs for a Belk department store, Big "C" Discount Drugs, Benson Furniture, The Pants Shop, and Pearle Vision Center.

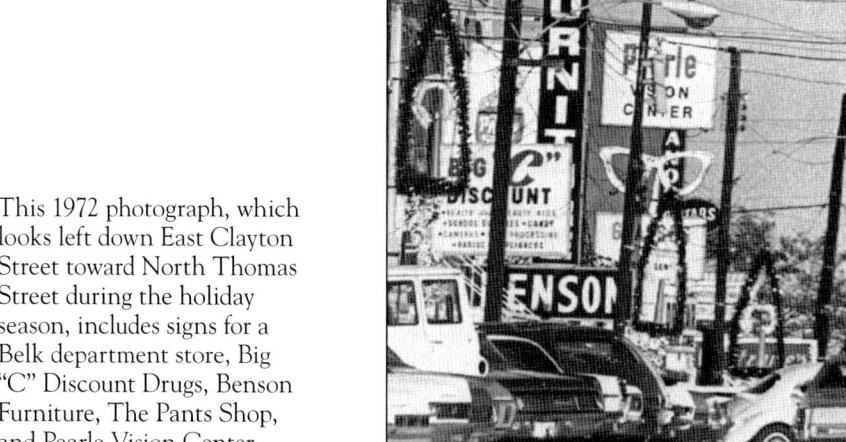

By 1974, at places like the Wrangler Steak House on College Avenue and Hoagie's Sandwich Shop on East Broad Street, patrons could finally be served what seems so common today: beer on tap at a downtown, student-friendly establishment.

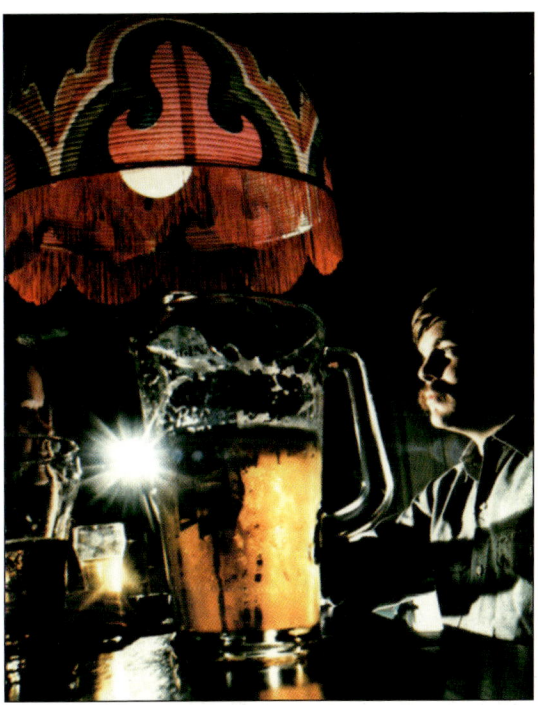

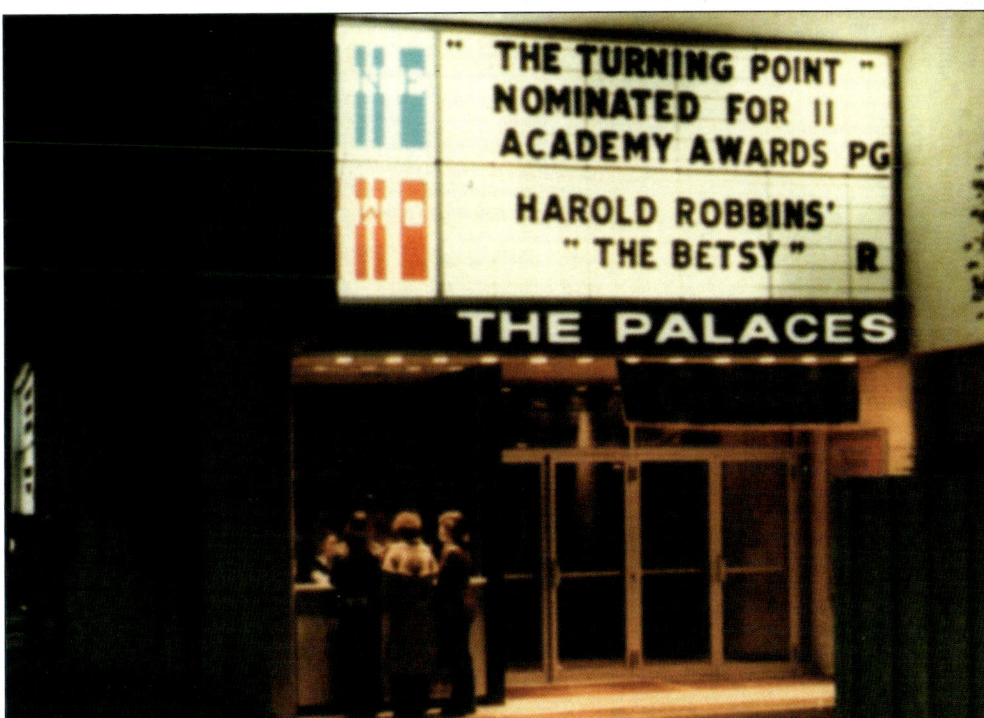

The Palace Theatre (later known as the Palace Twin), pictured here during the late 1970s, operated on College Avenue from 1921 until May 1987, when it was demolished. Closed (and razed) primarily because it could not compete with suburban theaters, the Palace Theatre was replaced with a parking deck.

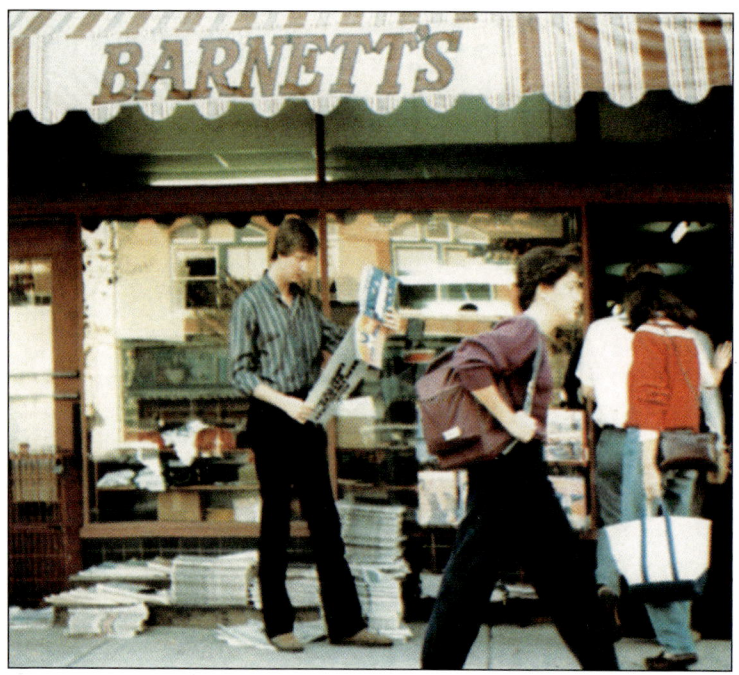

Barnett's News Stand, located on College Avenue, is bustling in this mid-1980s photograph. The old-fashioned newsstand and downtown landmark sold a variety of convenience items but also served as a social hub of sorts. It opened in 1942 and, after more than five decades of keeping Athenians informed, closed in 2008 because of declining sales and "a lot of red tape with the vendors," according to then-owner Midge Gray.

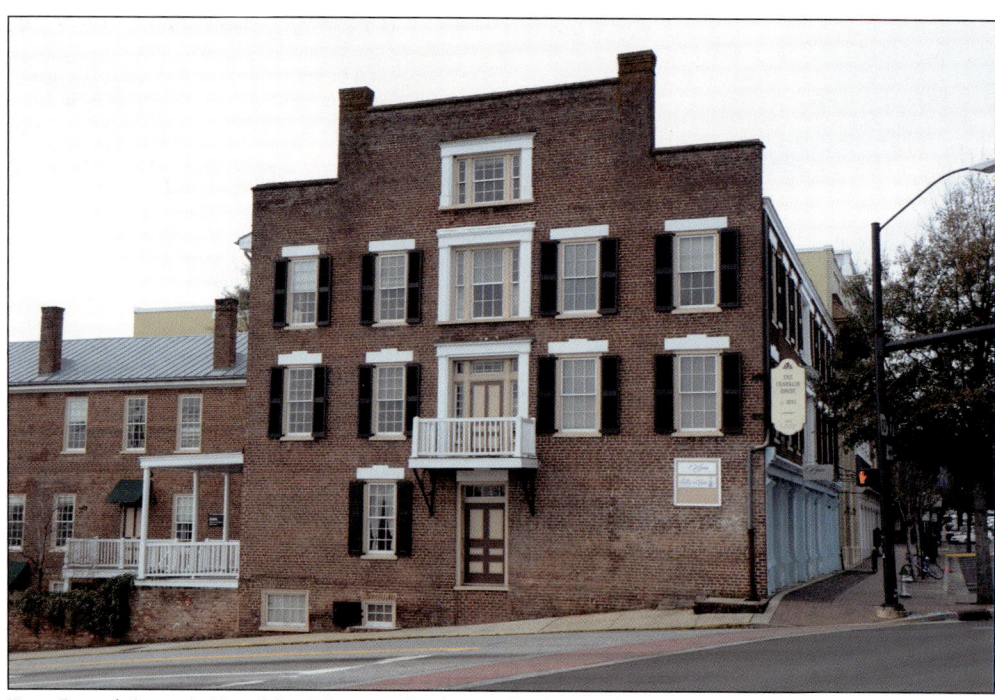

East Broad Street's Franklin House, which was built as a hotel in the 1840s and named after Benjamin Franklin, underwent a drastic renovation in the mid-1980s. A brokerage firm, which occupied three-quarters of the first floor and half of the second floor, was the house's first new tenant; it was soon followed by a bakery and a barbershop. (Courtesy of McGinnis Leathers.)

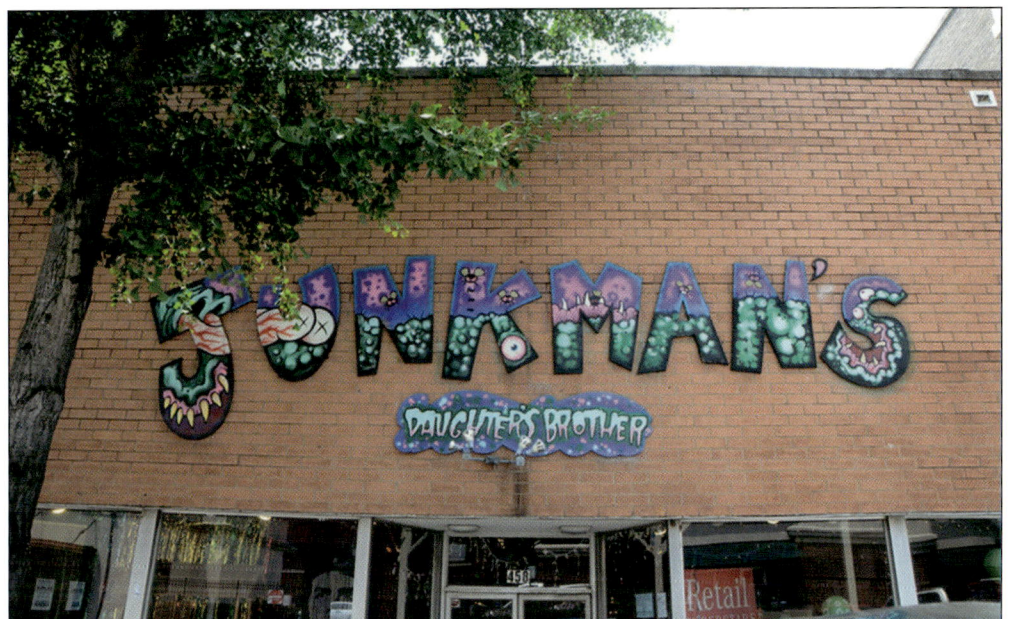

The "sibling" store of Atlanta's acclaimed Junkman's Daughter, Junkman's Daughter's Brother became an Athens landmark on East Clayton Street after it moved from the shop's original location on Broad Street in 1989. The eclectic novelty and costume shop spans more than 15,000 square feet and is the city's largest downtown business. In April 2014, owner Mark Gavron announced the upcoming closing of the store, which has been open since 1986, because he was ready for retirement. (Courtesy of McGinnis Leathers.)

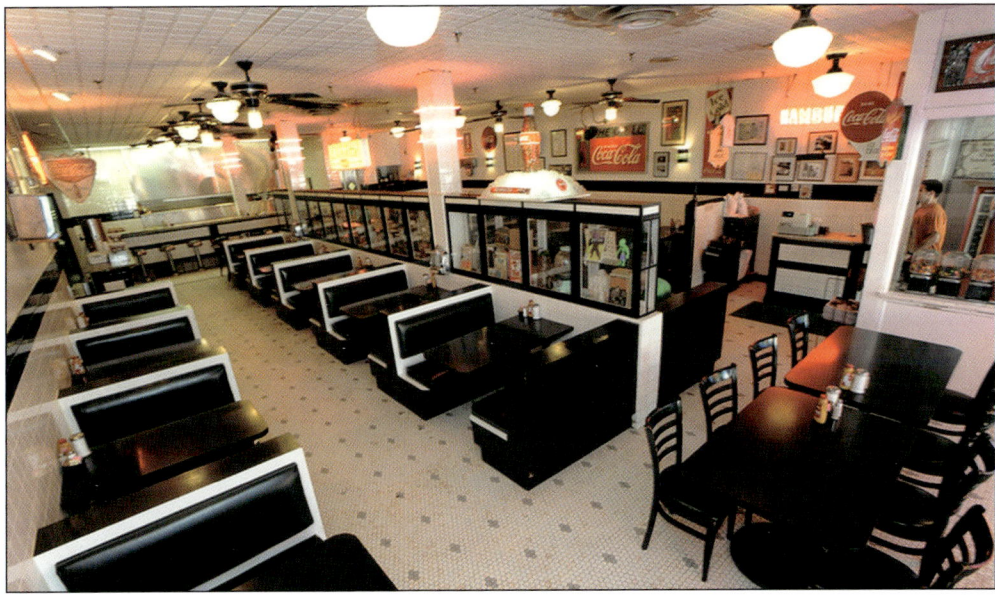

In the early 1980s, The Grill, which was then located on East Broad Street, was described as specializing in hamburgers, shakes, and fries in "a black-and-white New York atmosphere . . . makes you think you've walked into a Woody Allen movie." By the end of the decade, The Grill had moved to its current College Avenue location, where it has twice the capacity as before and serves as the only downtown restaurant open 24 hours a day. (Courtesy of McGinnis Leathers.)

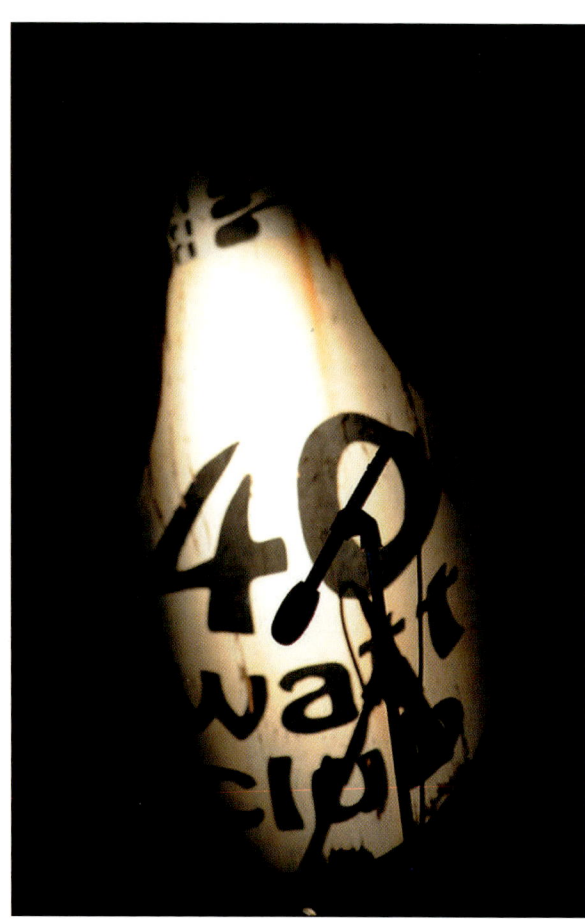

The 40 Watt Club, an iconic and world-renowned music venue, began in 1979 as a practice space for the band Pylon. The stage of the 40 Watt Club has been graced by the majority of Athens's most famous bands: R.E.M., the B-52's, the aforementioned Pylon, Drive-By Truckers, The Whigs, and more. Over the years, the acclaimed club has relocated four times. This image shows the stage at the 40 Watt's current location, 285 West Washington Street, where it has remained since April 1991. (Courtesy of McGinnis Leathers.)

On January 5, 1967, Curtis Smith, a former UGA student and member of the US Armed Forces, opened the Last Resort on 184 West Clayton Street—the first live-music club in Athens. By the 1980s, the Last Resort was "the most eclectic club in town." It became the Last Resort Grill by the early 1990s, transforming into a sophisticated bistro. (Courtesy of McGinnis Leathers.)

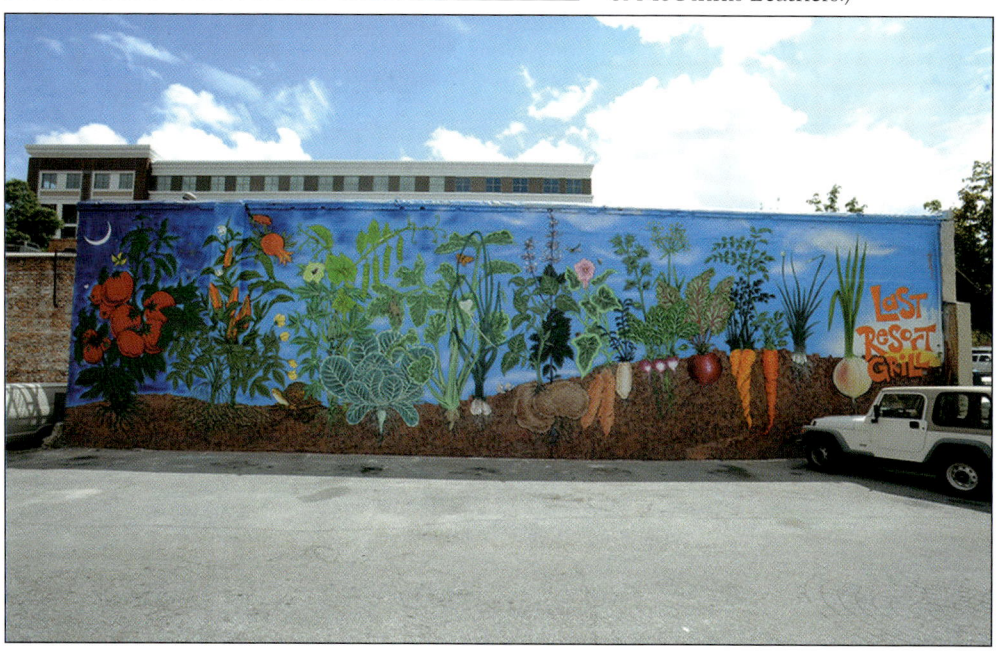

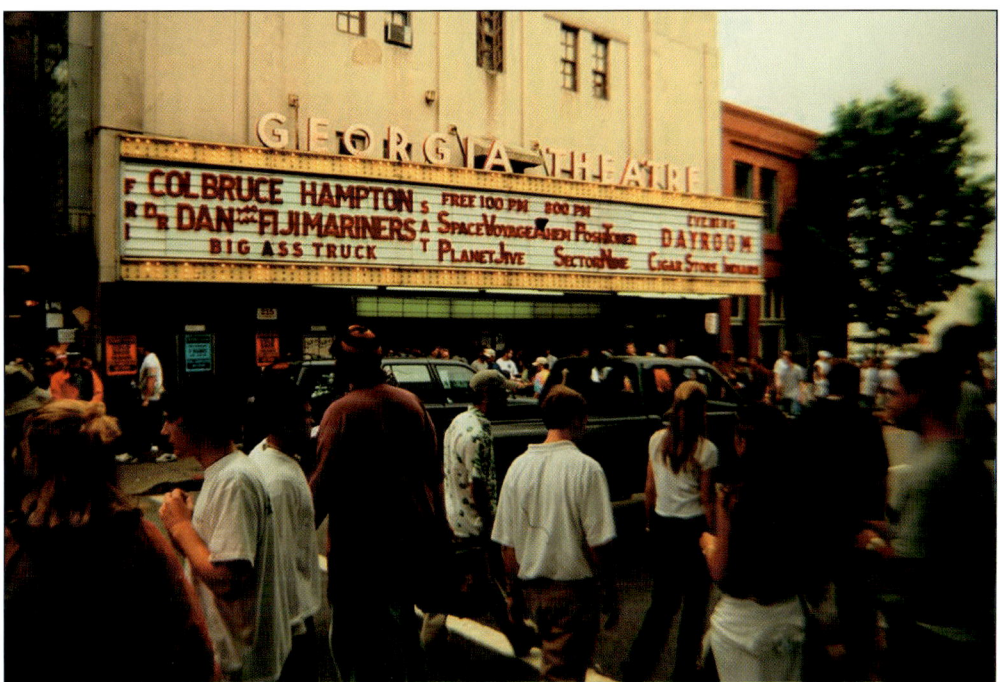

After serving as a concert hall for over a decade, the Georgia Theatre opened as a concert venue in the late 1980s with local band Pylon performing the first show. This 1990s photograph shows the "pre-fire" theater. On June 19, 2009, a major fire erupted in the facility, inflicting severe damage to the building and collapsing its roof. The Georgia Theatre was rebuilt after the fire and reopened in the same space on August 1, 2011. (Courtesy of Terry Allen.)

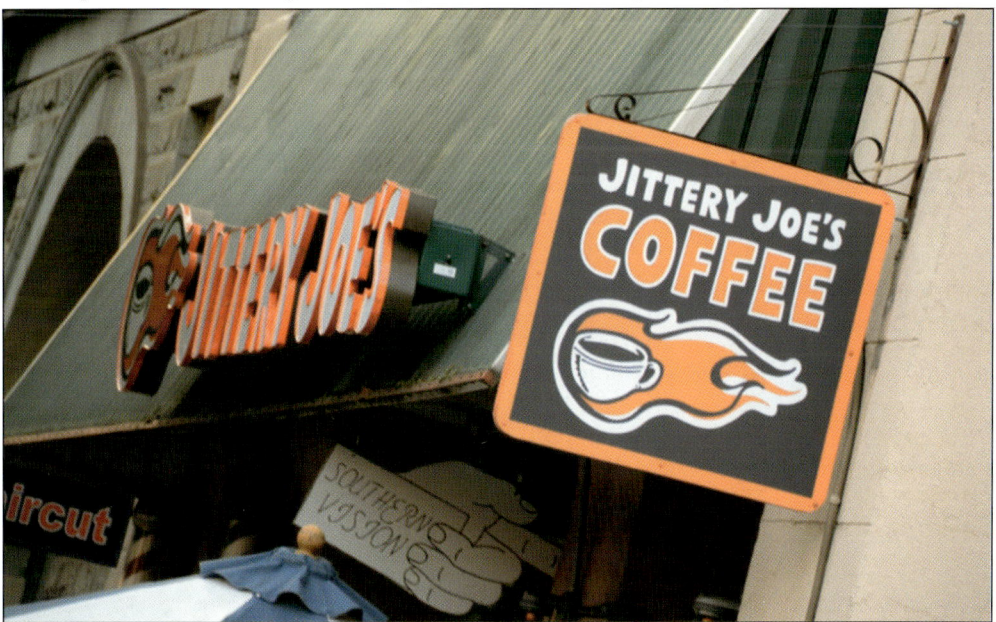

The first Jittery Joe's opened in May 1994 as a "non-alcoholic coffee bar" on West Washington Street. Twenty years later, the downtown location has since moved a half mile away, to East Broad Street, and there are now nine Jittery Joe's locations across Athens. (Courtesy of McGinnis Leathers.)

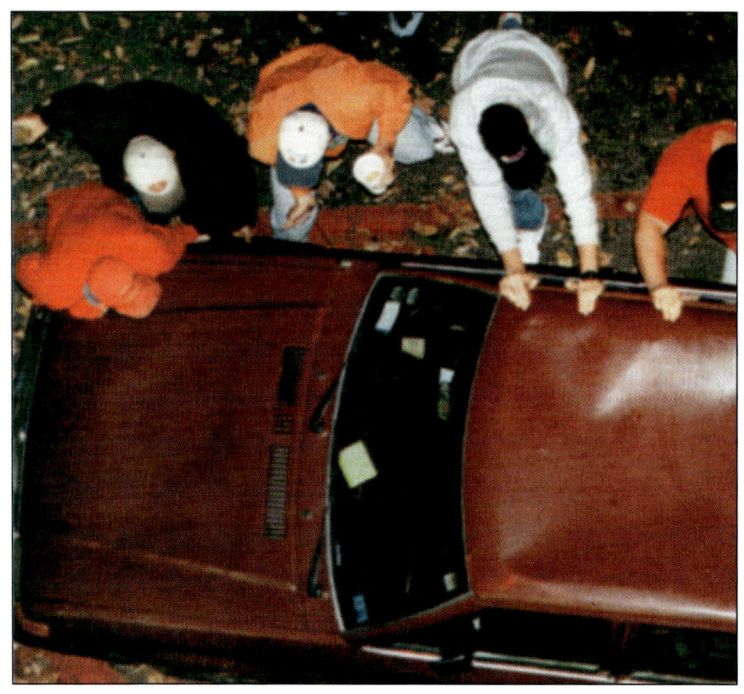

After the Atlanta Braves defeated the Cleveland Indians four games to two to clinch the 1995 World Series in Atlanta, the postgame excitement traveled at least 70 miles northeast, where Braves fans celebrated in downtown Athens. Other than a few individuals who were dropped while "crowd surfing" and this car getting turned over in front of the Georgia Theatre, the partying remained harmless.

In this mid-1990s photograph, a couple of "townies" check out some CDs at Wuxtry Records on East Clayton Street. Since 1976, Wuxtry has served Athens as one of the oldest record-store chains in the state. Upstairs from Wuxtry is Bizarro-Wuxtry, which, according to the shop, sells "a vast assortment of crazy crap," including comics, magazines, art books, and toys.

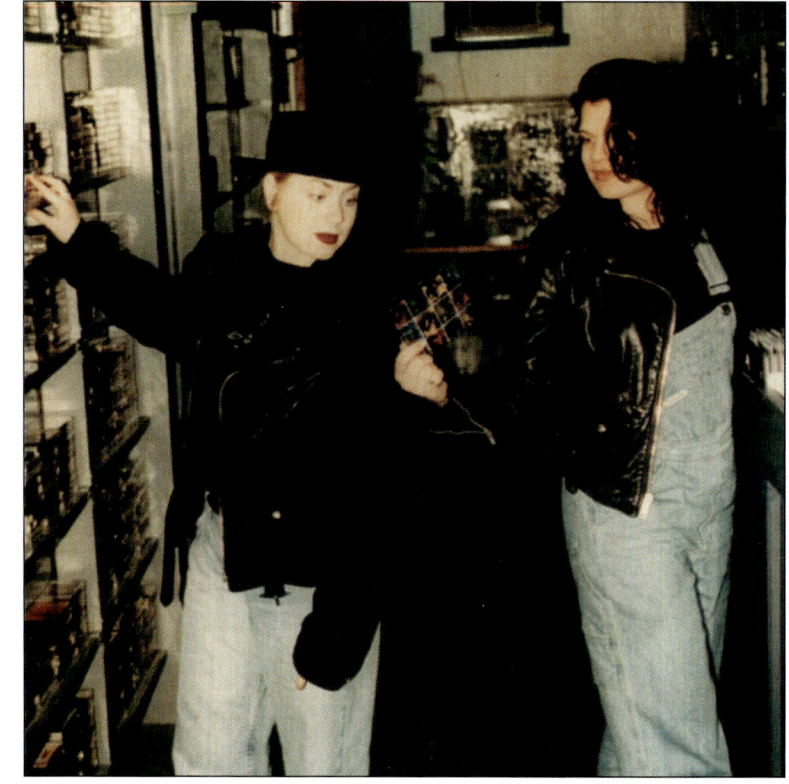

Just in time for the 1996–1997 academic year, The Armadillo opened on East Clayton Street, filling a vacancy in the downtown bar scene by catering to those fond of country music. Unfortunately, The Armadillo did not attract much of a following, as the establishment closed within a few years after its opening.

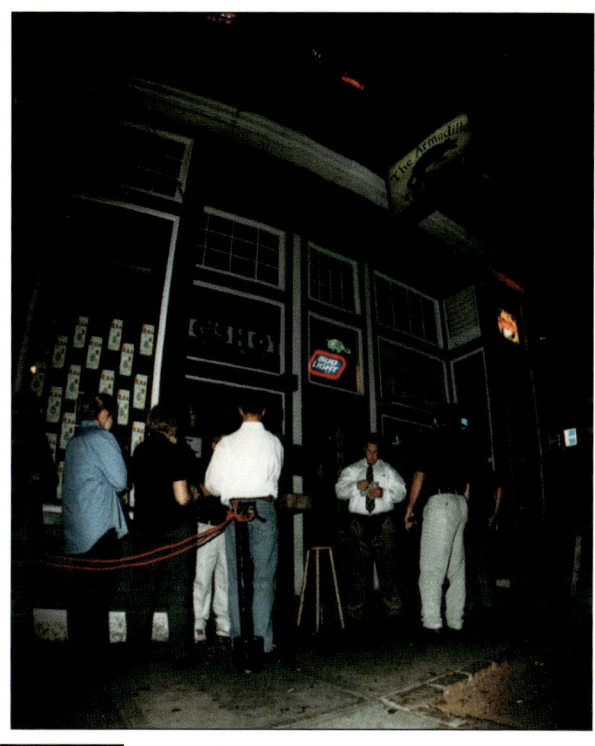

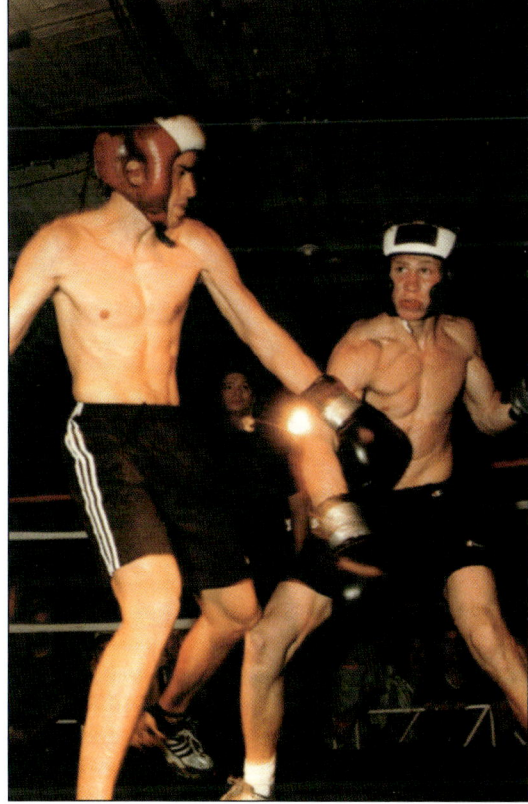

During the late 1990s, boxing became almost as big a deal at the 40 Watt Club as the bands that played at the downtown music venue. For a few years, both men and women participated in the Athens Boxing Championships in the spring and the Athens Fall Classic Boxing Tournament in the fall until the events were KO'd in 1999 due to a lack of interest.

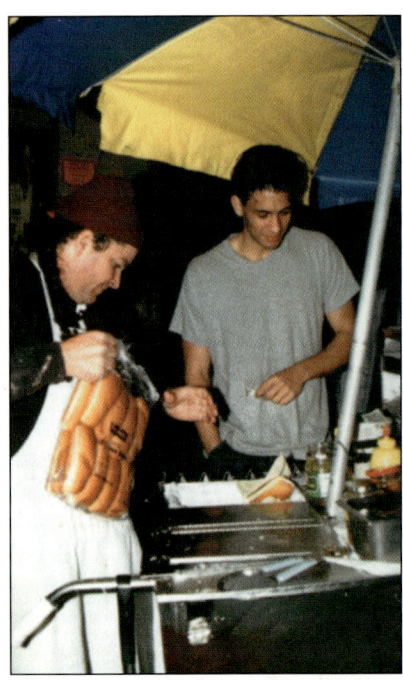

After the failure of his deli business in 1987, John Gundaker (left) grew his hair long and "decided to go back to the roots of this town, to deal with the students," as Gundaker said in 1995. For nearly 20 years, he operated as the "original" hot dog man in Athens, owning as many as five stands. In 2005, Gundaker's on-campus stands were shut down when UGA officials declared they "posed a danger to student traffic."

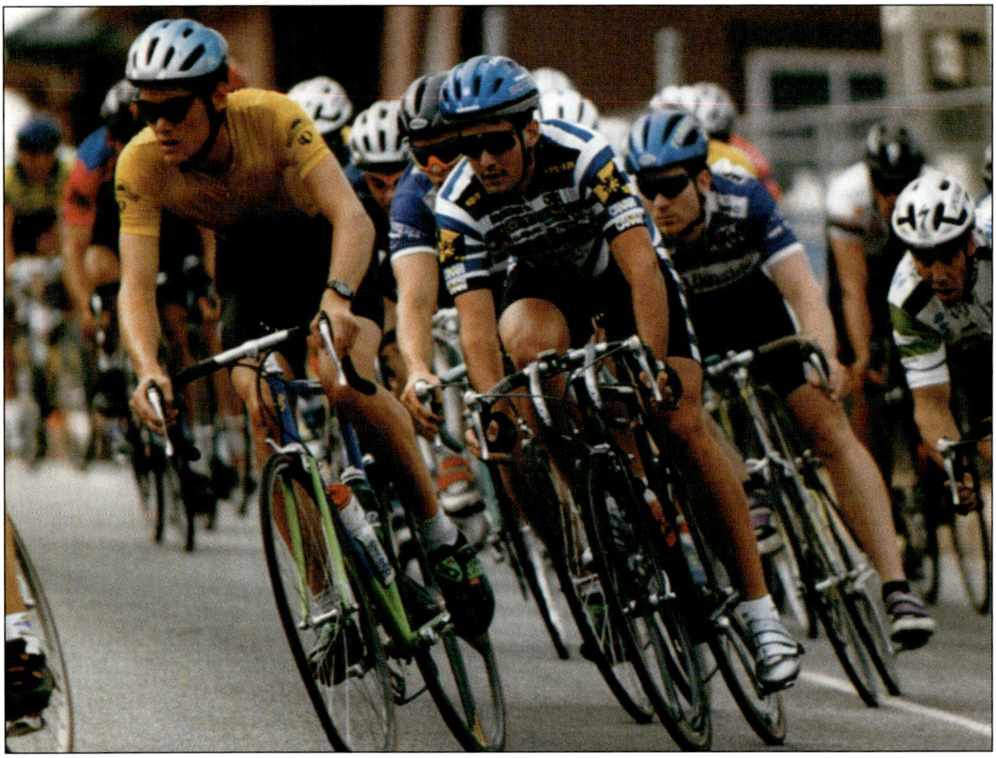

The Athens Twilight Criterium, which began with one nighttime bicycle race and 40 competitors, was founded in 1980. More than 30 years later, it has grown to offer eight separate race classes and has 150 cyclists competing in the main event. This image shows the event in the late 1990s, which was around the time separate winners were declared for both men's and women's groups.

The Widespread Panic concert held downtown in April 1998 attracted concertgoers and vendors, including this man selling "shroom" paraphernalia, from all over the country. City officials planned on a crowd of around 25,000 but were prepared to handle 40,000; instead, as many as 100,000 people turned out for the show. "[The crowd] mushroomed into something much larger than what was originally understood," said then-Athens-Clarke County manager Al Crace.

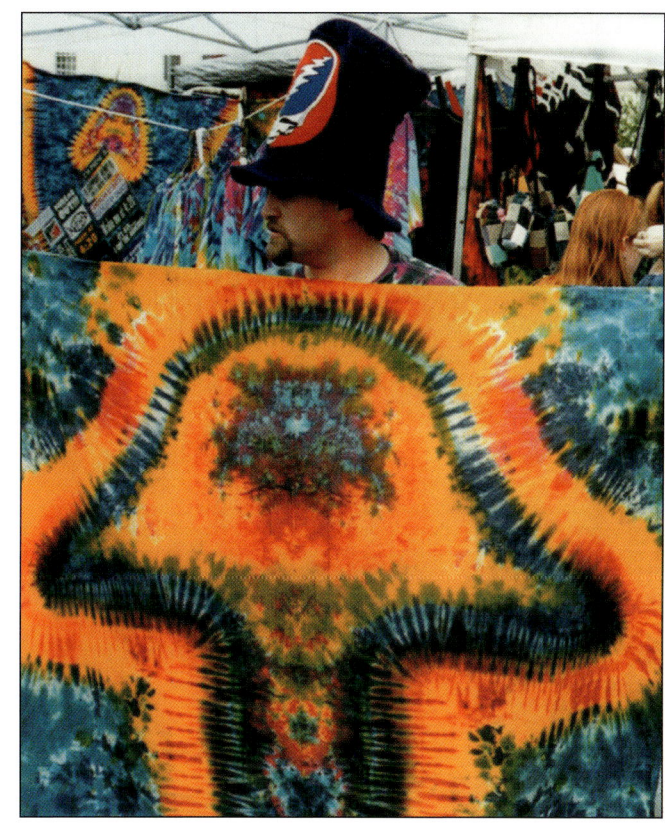

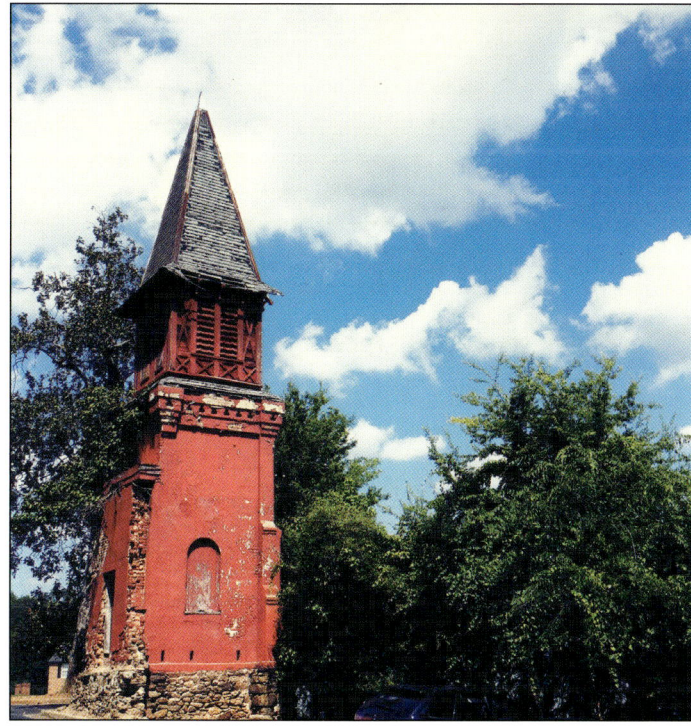

This church steeple at 376 Oconee Street once sat next to a 108-year-old, two-story brick church linked to the most famous bands of Athens, including R.E.M., which held rehearsals inside the church in 1979. On November 30, 1999, a fire severely damaged the building, and the church was decimated, leaving behind the landmark known as the "R.E.M. steeple." (Courtesy of McGinnis Leathers.)

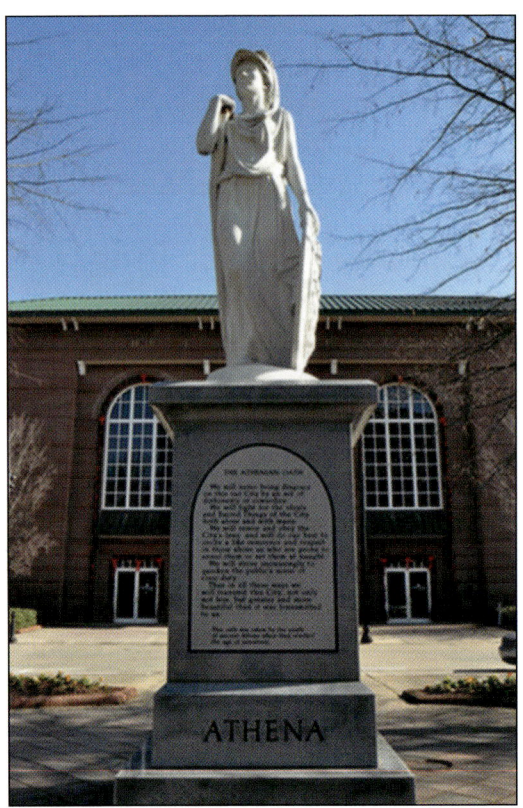

In 1996, the Classic Center opened as northeast Georgia's premier convention center and performing arts venue. The first performance at the center was the Broadway musical *Cats*. That same year, the statue of Athena was unveiled to stand outside the center and face downtown. The Greek goddess of wisdom symbolizes the city's namesake: Athens, Greece. (Courtesy of McGinnis Leathers.)

George Walker Dean (left) was the owner of George Dean's Men's Store on East Clayton Street beginning in 1966, when he bought the long-standing John Q. West apparel shop. George is pictured here in 2001 with his son Wayne Dean. George was a fixture of downtown Athens. Today, Wayne continues the family tradition of operating George Dean's, which has been known for decades as a place to shop for fine men's clothing in Athens. (Courtesy of Wayne Dean.)

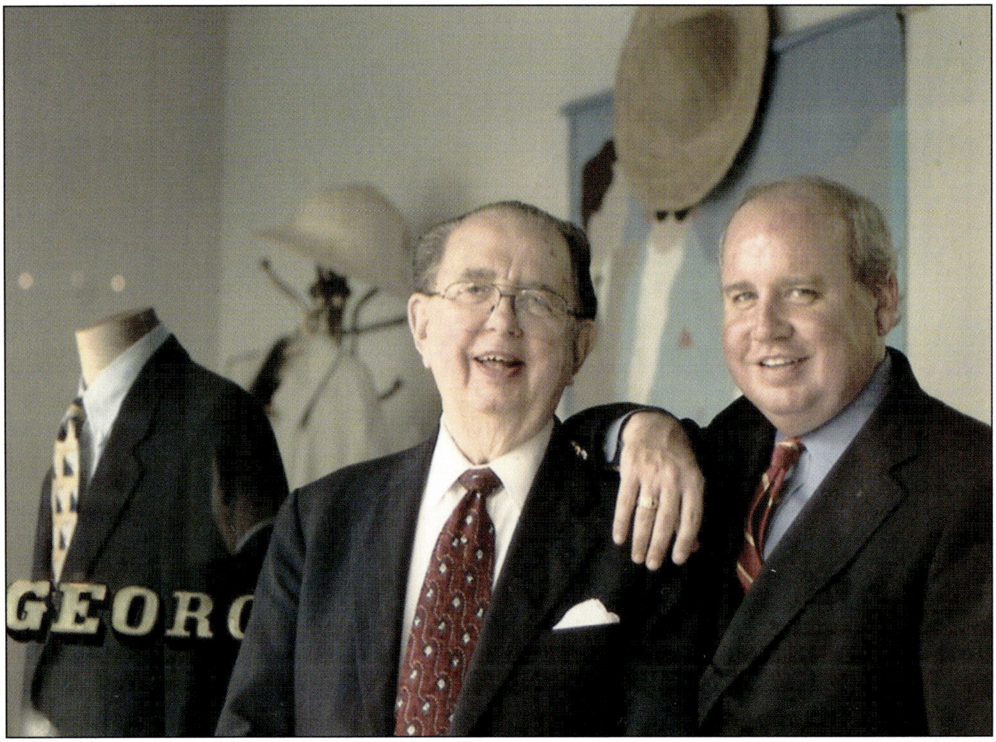

In the wake of the September 11 attacks, an impromptu memorial—consisting of candles, poems, T-shirts, and other items—arose on the steps of the UGA Arch, where people could gather and remember the victims. The US flag was placed on the Arch, marking what is believed to be the first time the university gave express permission for something to be hung on its Arch.

AthFest, founded in 1997, began as a two-day annual music event held during the summer in downtown Athens. By June 2013, its 16th year, the festival had expanded to become a free, five-day annual music and arts festival featuring 150 bands and selected by the Southeast Tourism Society as one of the top 20 regional events held in June. Here, Athens band Dreams So Real performs at a fairly recent AthFest. (Courtesy of Terry Allen.)

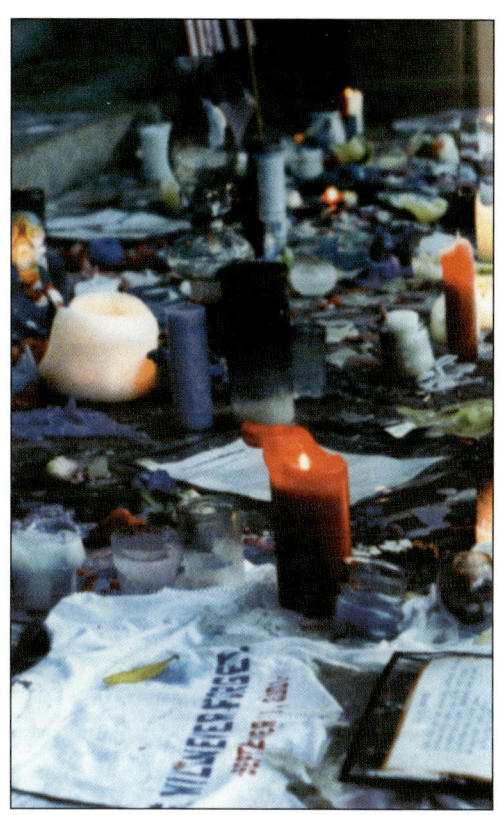

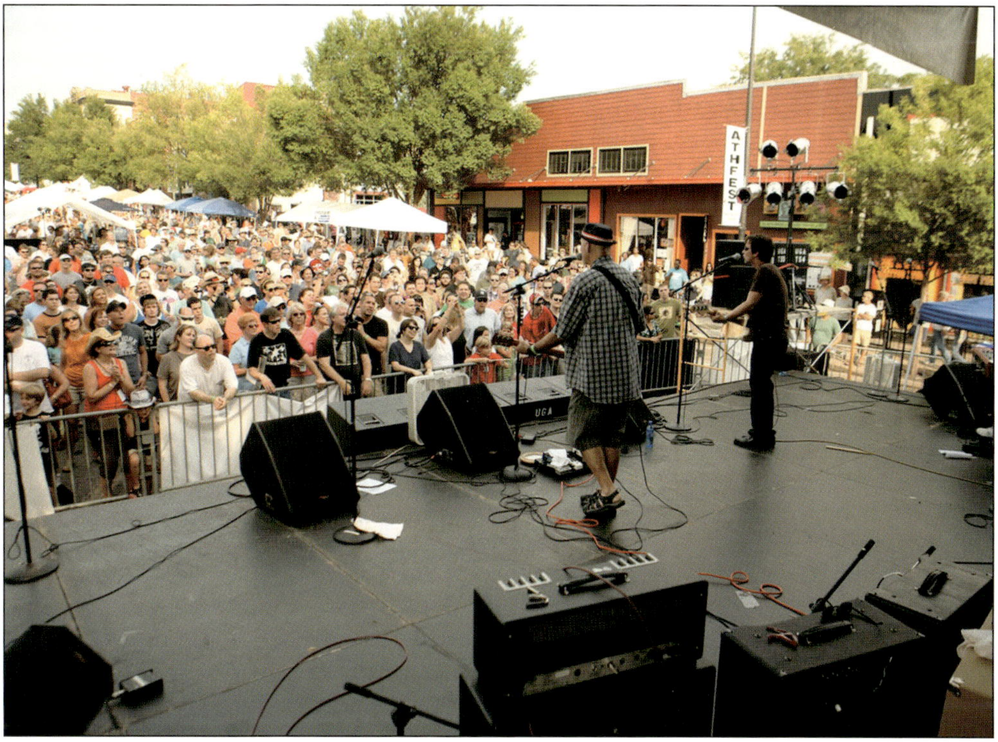

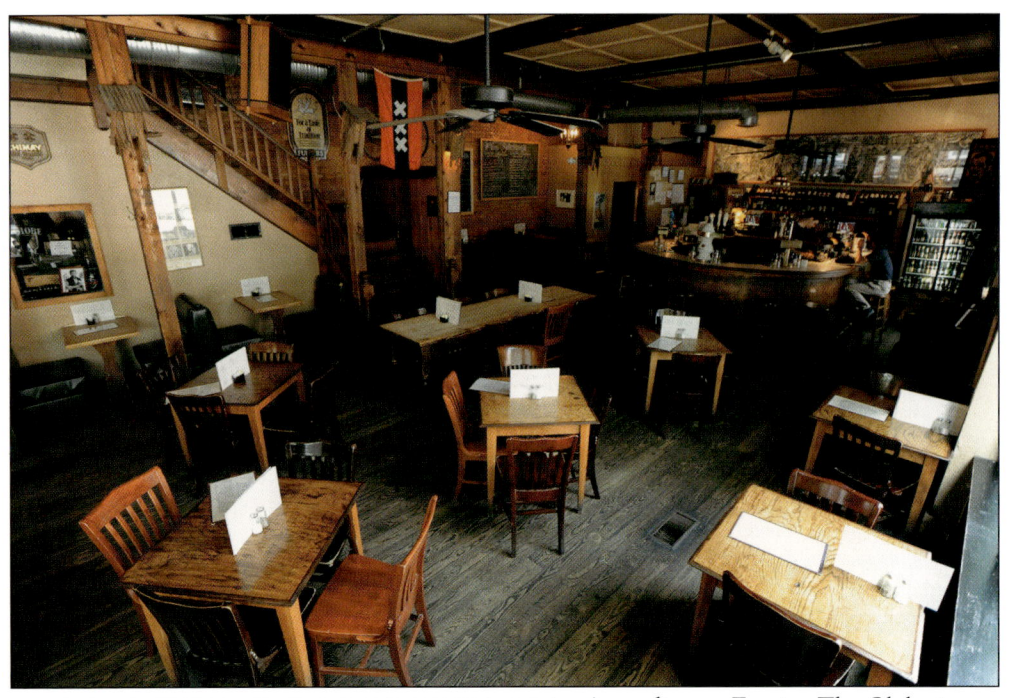

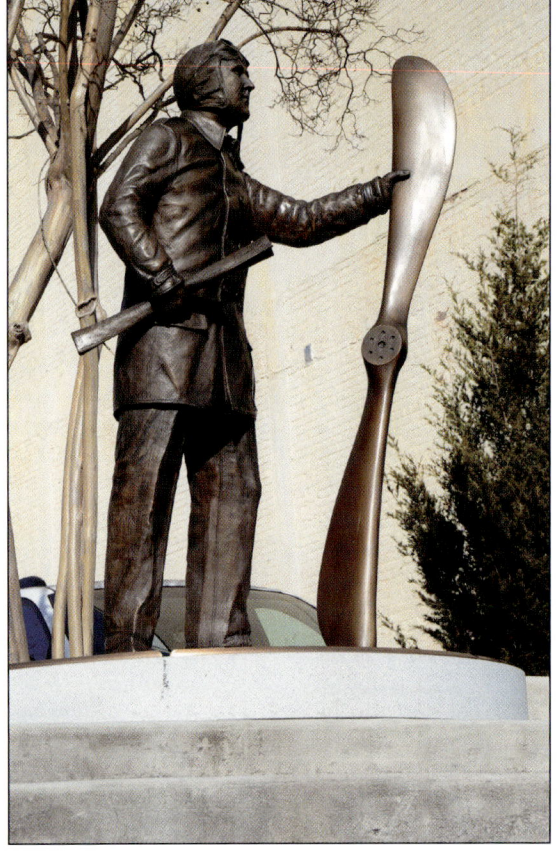

According to *Esquire*, The Globe is where "rowdy undergrads reign during the fall and spring semesters" and "grad students and locals drink early evenings away during the summer." In 2007, *Esquire* voted the bar on North Lumpkin Street as the third-best bar in the United States. The Globe is known for its wide range of tasty microbrews and imports served at a well-designed and inviting bar. (Courtesy of McGinnis Leathers.)

Oconee County native Ben Epps built and flew the first airplane in Athens in 1907. Over 100 years later, a statue of Epps was erected on East Washington Street directly across the street from the location of Epps's original garage. (Courtesy of McGinnis Leathers.)

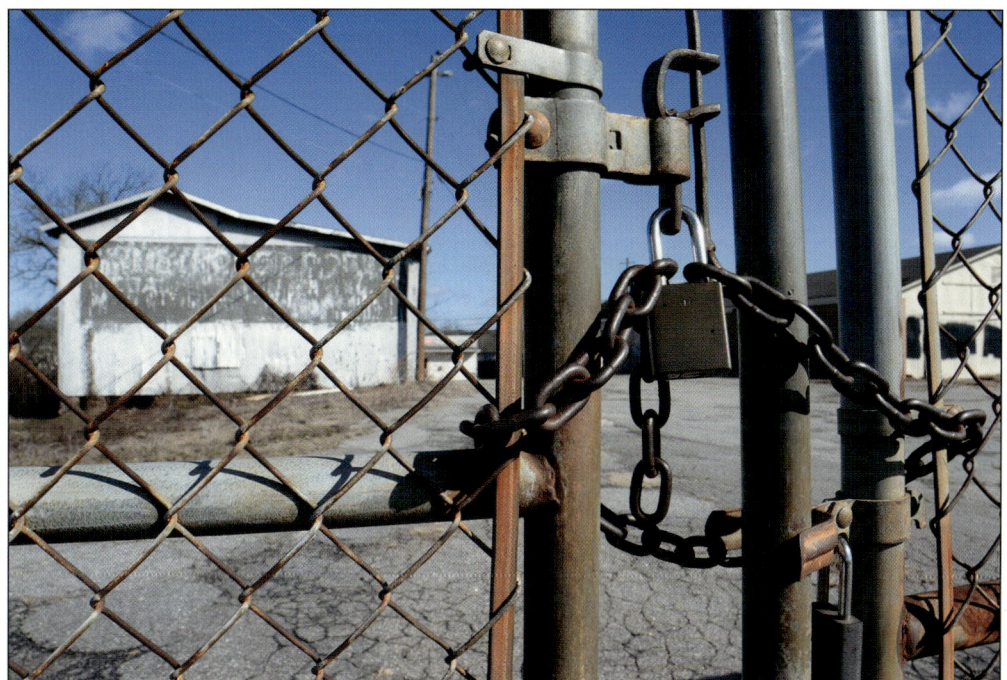

This image shows the space between Oconee and East Broad Streets where a major mixed-use development—including a downtown Walmart—was once proposed, with the mega-retailer to serve as the anchor tenant. However, many thousands of current and former Athens residents opposed the idea, and in December 2012, the developer, Selig Enterprises, decided to nix the project. (Courtesy of McGinnis Leathers.)

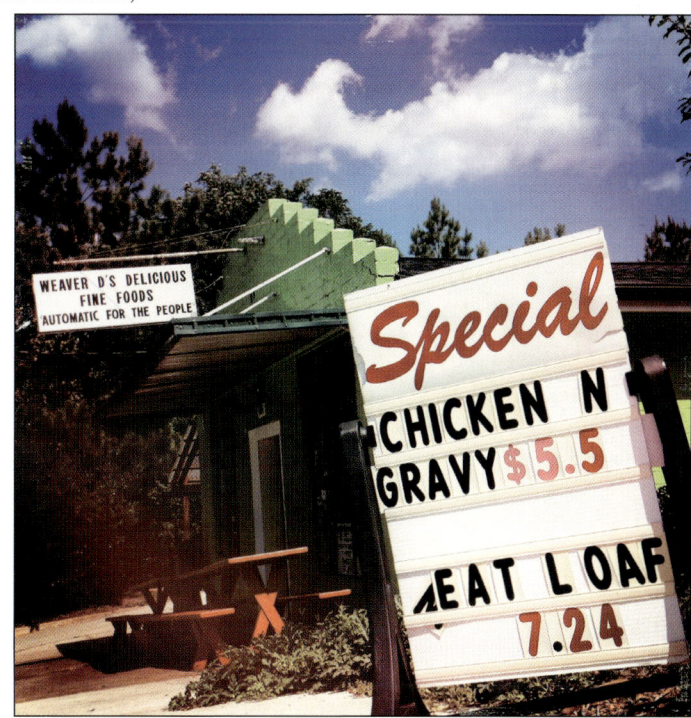

Located on the edge of downtown Athens, Weaver D's Fine Foods has been one of Athens's favorite restaurants for nearly 30 years. Besides his delicious food, owner Dexter Weaver is best known for his slogan, "automatic for the people," which R.E.M. used as the title of their Grammy-nominated 1992 album. Weaver D's nearly closed in 2012, and then again in November 2013, but as of 2014 the restaurant, fortunately, remains open. Automatic. (Courtesy of McGinnis Leathers.)

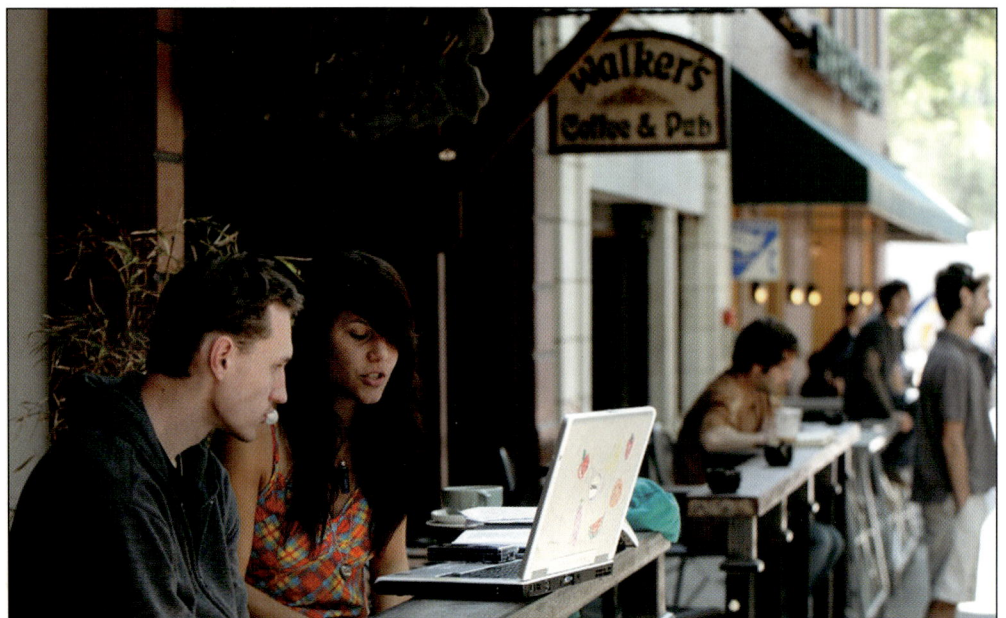

As of 2014, there were roughly 80 bars and dozens of coffee houses in downtown Athens, including places where one could grab both a drink and a unique roasted coffee, like Walker's Coffee and Pub on College Avenue. This is a sharp contrast to just a few decades before, when there were hardly any bars in the downtown district and coffee was primarily served only in restaurants. (Courtesy of Terry Allen.)

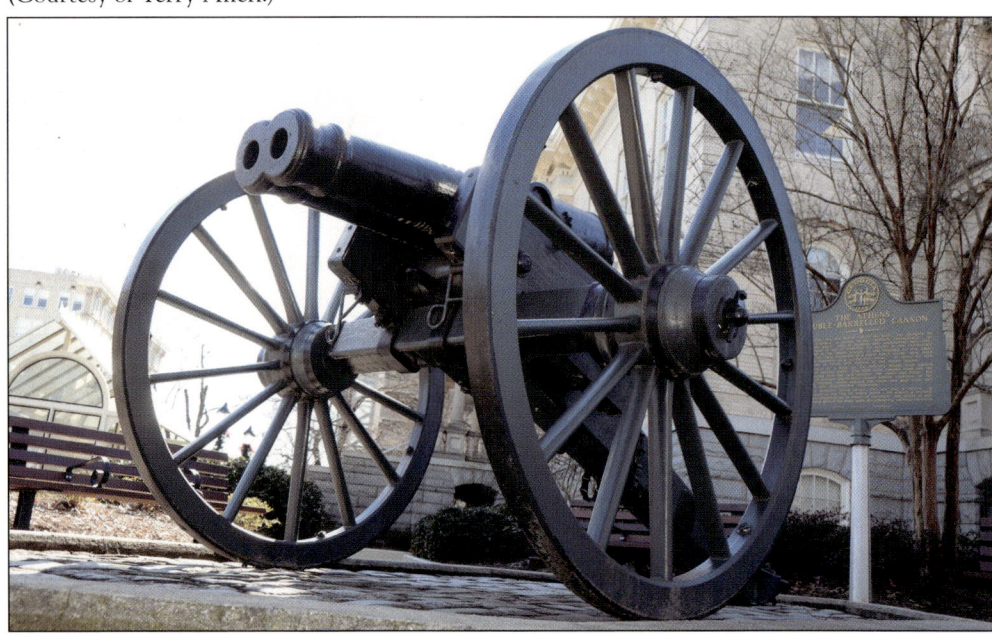

The famous double-barreled cannon—one of Athens' most prized possessions—was originally cast at the Athens Steam Company in 1862. More than 150 years later, it now stands on the lawn of city hall. Featured in *Ripley's Believe It or Not!*, the inoperative cannon is believed to be the only full-sized double-barrel cannon in existence. Just in case it suddenly becomes functional, the cannon is pointed north, away from downtown Athens. (Courtesy of McGinnis Leathers.)

Four

How 'Bout Them Dogs?

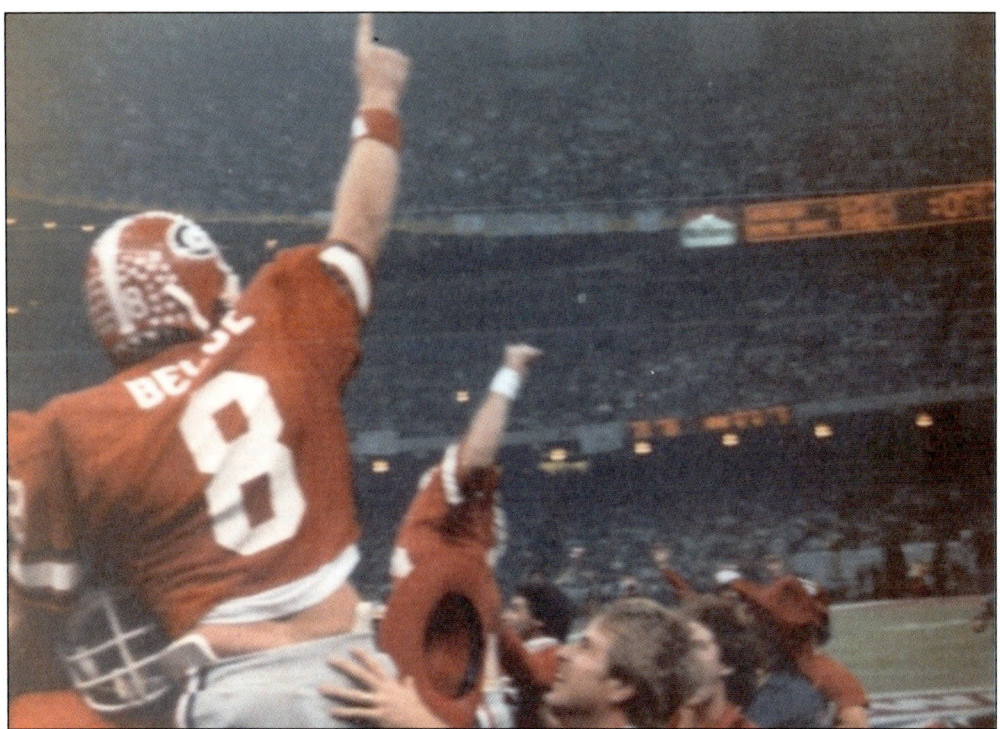

This image captures what was arguably the greatest moment in the history of UGA athletics: the Georgia football team's defeat of Notre Dame in the 1981 Sugar Bowl to claim the national championship. Although the title was clinched in New Orleans, the battle cry of "How 'Bout Them Dogs!" could be heard around the nation, especially in Athens, where Bulldog fans partied in the streets for hours following the historic moment. (Courtesy of Rob Saye.)

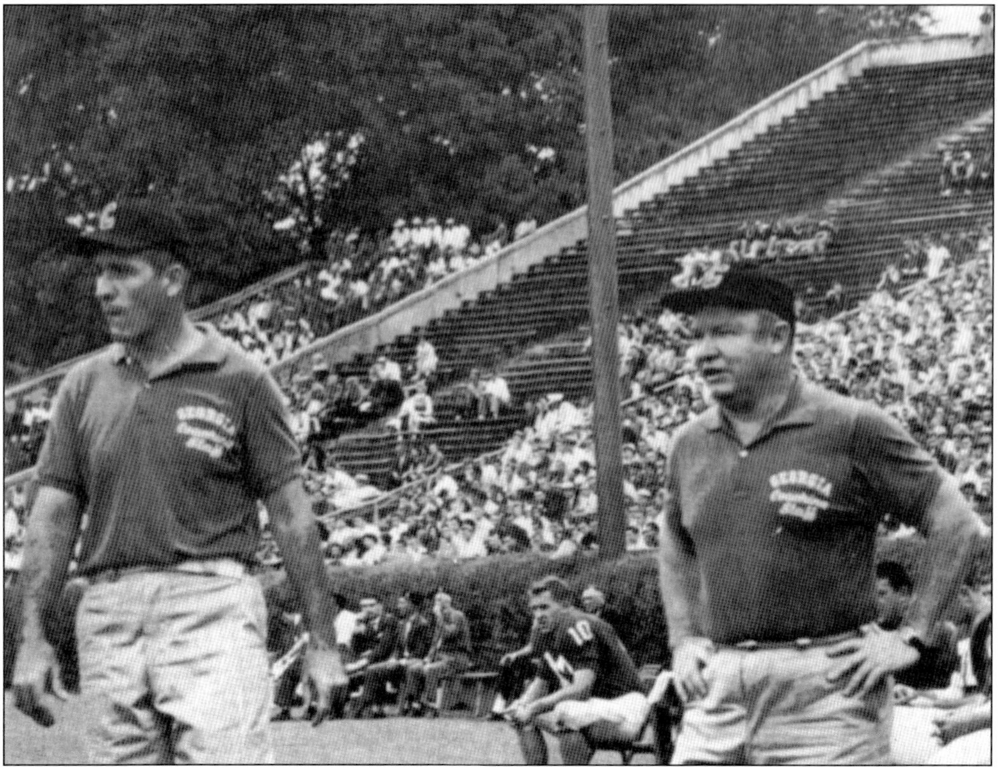

Following a successful tenure as UGA's head football coach and while serving as athletic director, Wally Butts (right) was alleged by *The Saturday Evening Post* in 1963 to have given "significant secrets" regarding the Bulldogs, who were then coached by Johnny Griffith, to Alabama head coach Paul "Bear" Bryant prior to the teams' meeting in 1962. Charley Trippi (left), a UGA athletics legend and an assistant under Butts, served as the "star" witness for his old coach in a libel suit trial, in which Butts won.

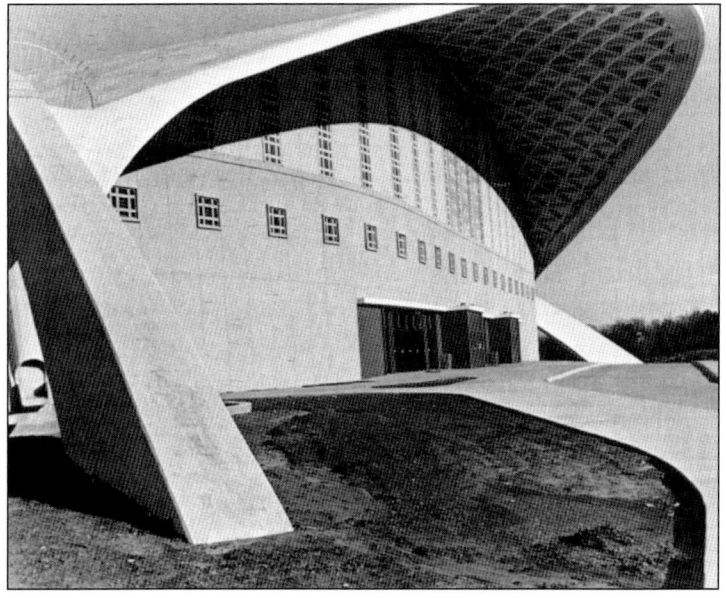

The Georgia Coliseum is pictured here shortly after its grand opening in 1964. Built to serve as an all-purpose arena, the Coliseum has hosted much more than UGA basketball, concerts, and rodeos—it was equipped with its own stage and livestock stables. In 1996, the arena was dedicated to the memory of former UGA athletics icon Herman James Stegeman and renamed Stegeman Coliseum.

For over 100 years, the chapel bell located on UGA's North Campus has been rung by fans following each football victory. Exactly when the ritual started is a matter of debate; the newest claim, discovered in 2014, declares that the tradition began after a 10-8 win over Auburn in 1894. The photograph at right shows several Georgia fans ringing the bell following a victory over Kentucky in 1958. The image below shows a young Bulldogs fan ringing the bell after Georgia's win over Tennessee in 2012. (Below, courtesy of Nigel Bynum.)

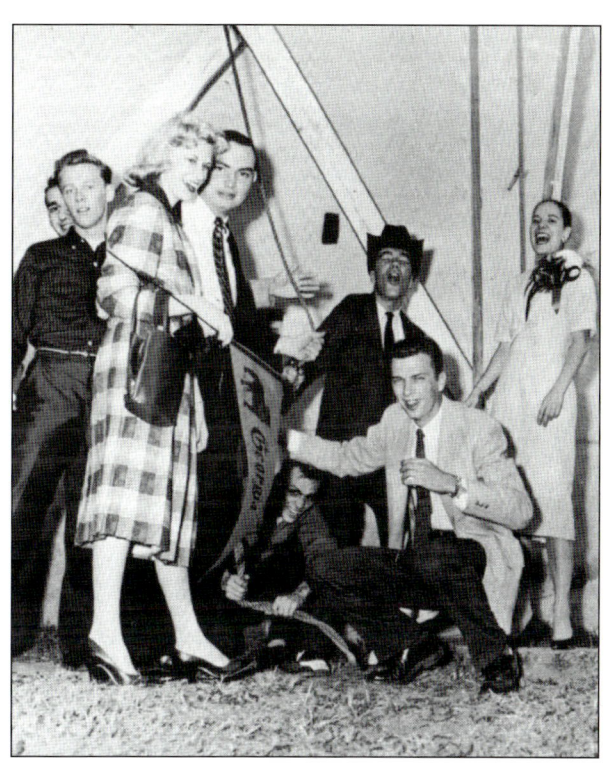

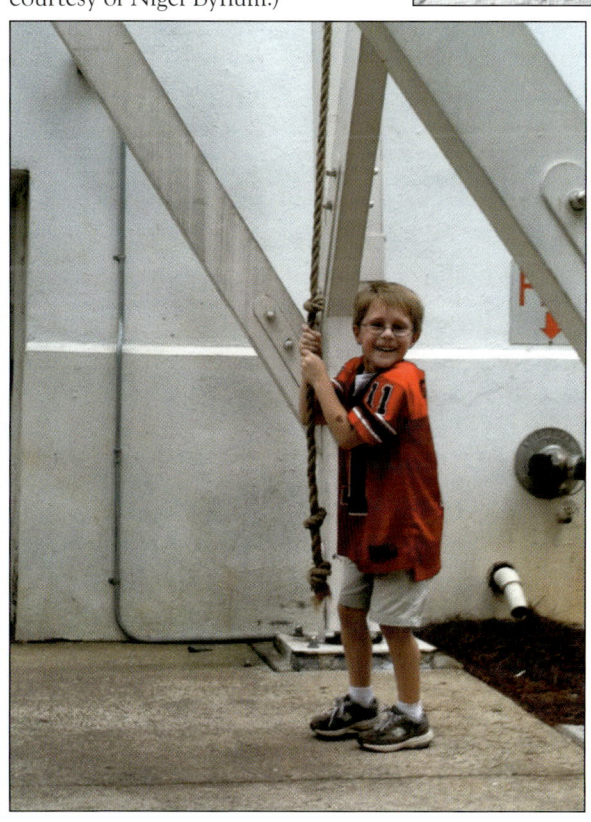

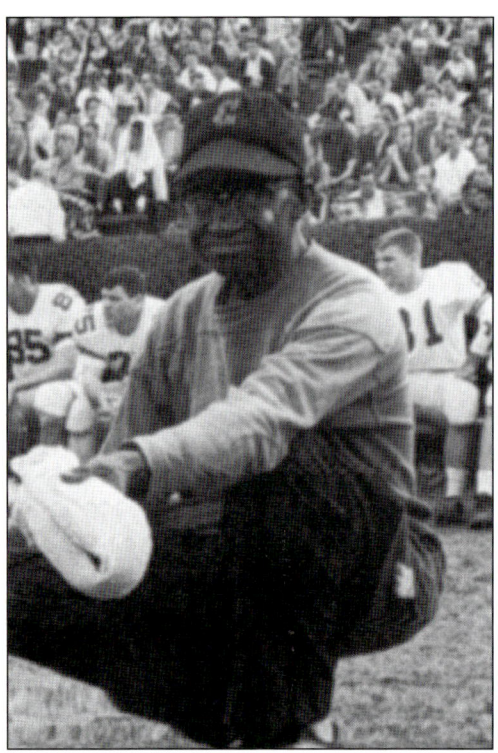

Pleasant Stark, better known as "Clegg," became UGA football's "official mascot" during the 1910s. For approximately the next 50 years, Stark worked for the athletic department in some capacity—including as the football team's famous water boy—until his death in 1964. Alumni tell a story of how Stark was once able to throw a football from one goal post through the bars of the other post at the opposite end of the field.

In June 1969, Ronnie Hogue, from Washington, DC, signed a grant-in-aid to attend UGA, becoming the first African American to earn a major-sport athletic scholarship at the university. The small forward-shooting guard averaged nearly 18 points per game during his Georgia career (1971–1973), became the second Bulldog in history to tally 1,000 career points, earned first-team All-SEC honors in 1972, and set a single-game school record with his 46 points against LSU in 1971.

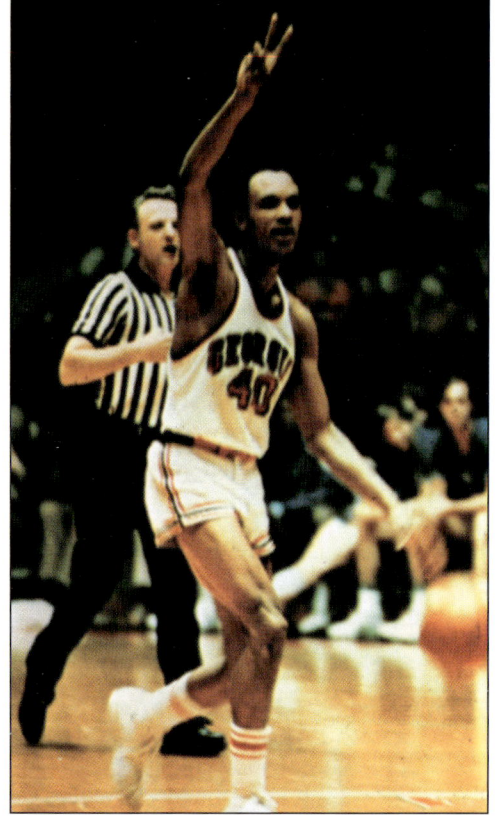

Quarterback Andy Johnson (center) discusses strategy with offensive coordinator Fred Pancoast (left) and Vince Dooley (right) during the 1971 Auburn game. Johnson, who led Athens High School to a state championship in 1969, won 25 games as the Bulldogs' starting quarterback from 1971 to 1973. Dooley won 201 games as the team's head coach from 1964 to 1988, becoming a coaching legend and an Athens icon in the process.

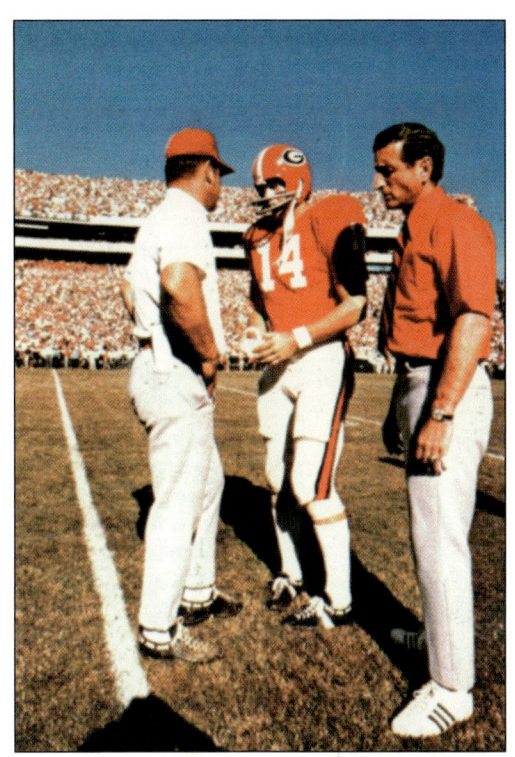

In 1975, when Georgia football's "picture day" was literally held on the field of Sanford Stadium, players Robert Wilson (left), Steve Davis (No. 80), and Ralph Page (No. 18) have some fun with mascot Uga III during the summer event. Since then, picture day has been held at a number of places, including as "fan day" in a recent return to Sanford Stadium, where the event is held inside the stadium but not on its field. (Courtesy of Helen Castronis.)

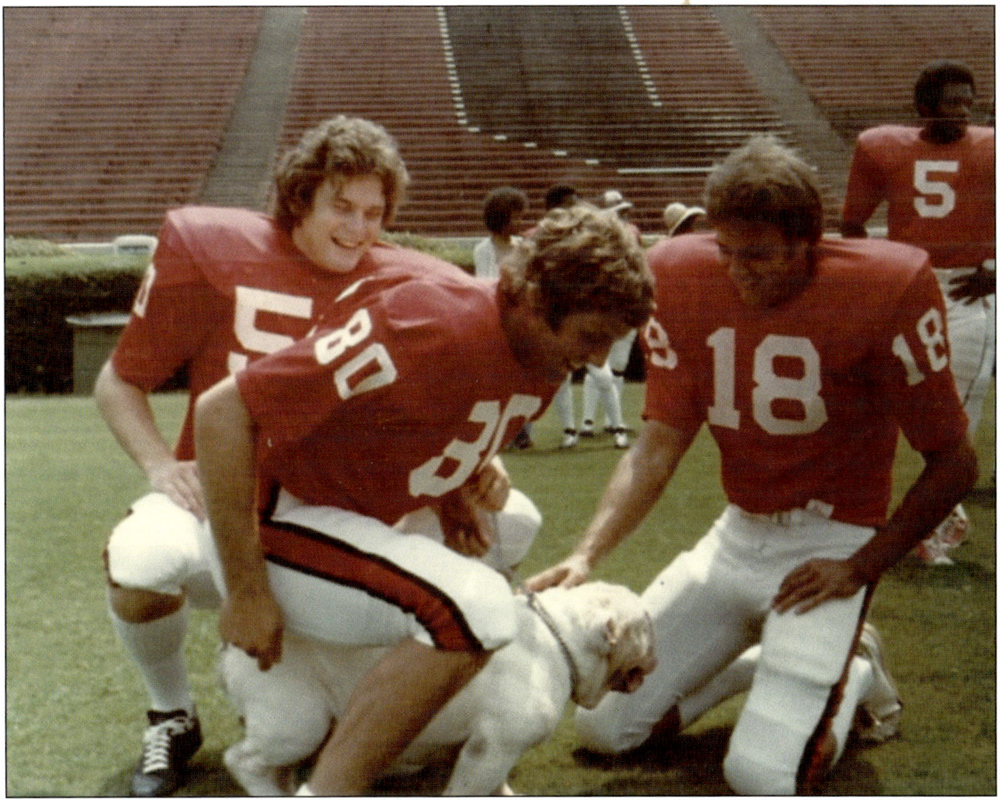

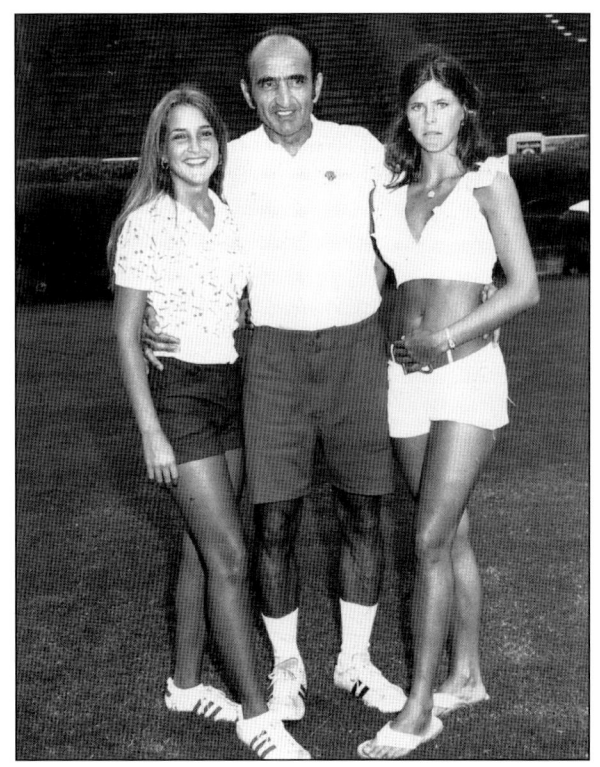

Georgia football fans Helen Castronis (left) and Sharon Hahne pose at left with Mike Castronis and below with Craig "Sky" Hertwig around 1973. Mike, Helen's father, was a revered man in Athens who served the university in several capacities during his lifetime, including as an assistant football coach. Hahne eventually married UGA football player Dick Conn, a standout defensive back. Hertwig was also a standout player—a 1974 first-team All-American—who stood six feet, eight inches high (thus the nickname "Sky"). After retiring from the NFL, Hertwig returned to Athens, where he ran local establishments the Fifth Quarter, Sky's Place, and the Odyssey. (Both, courtesy of Helen Castronis.)

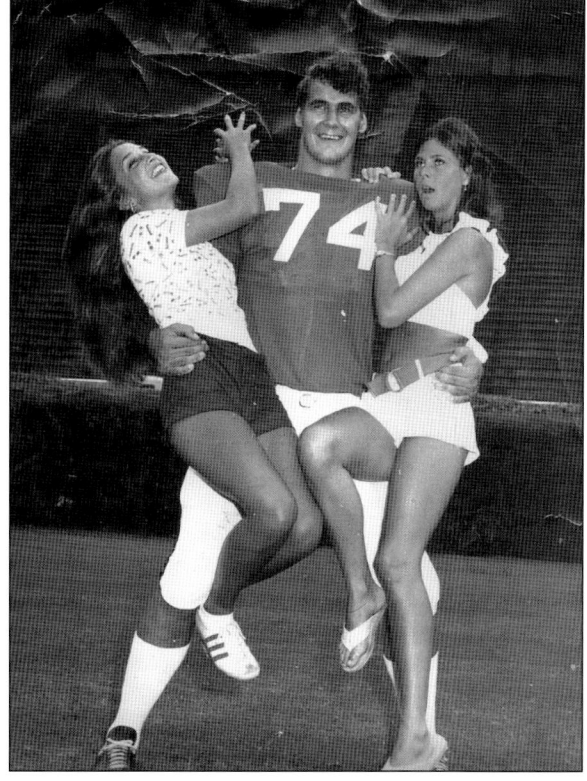

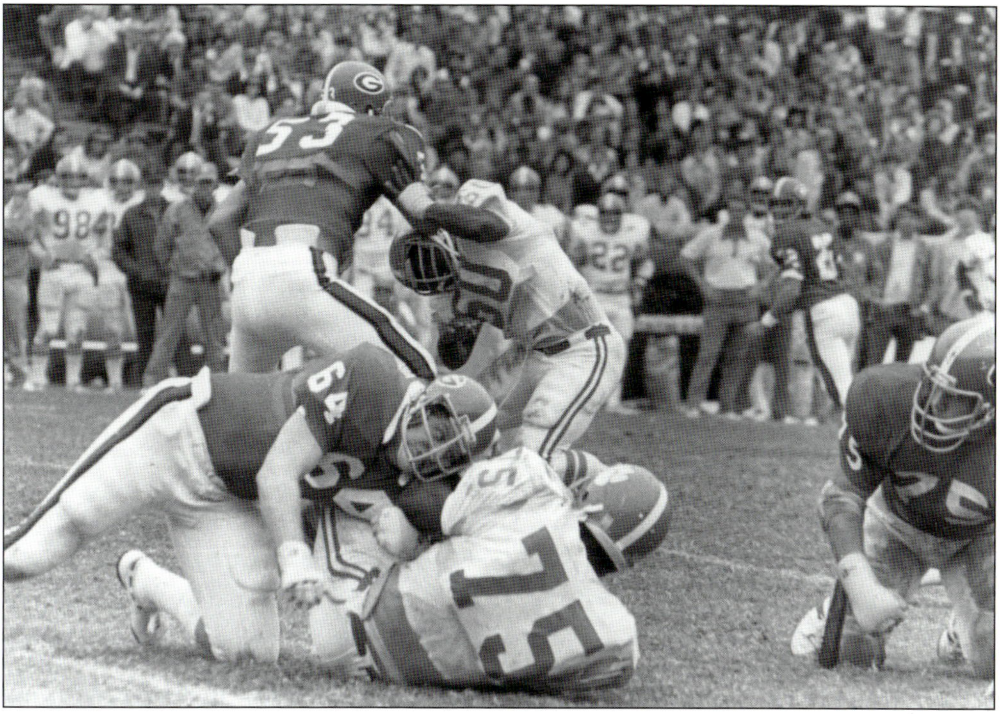

Bulldogs Ken Helms (No. 53), Hugh Hendrix (No. 64), and Steve Wilson (No. 75) block as Butch Box (No. 22) runs a pass route during a 35-7 rout of Clemson in 1975. From the mid-1970s through the late 1980s, there was perhaps no bigger football rival for Georgia than the Clemson Tigers. From 1974 through 1987, the Bulldogs won seven meetings, the Tigers won six, and there was one tie. (Courtesy of Ken Helms.)

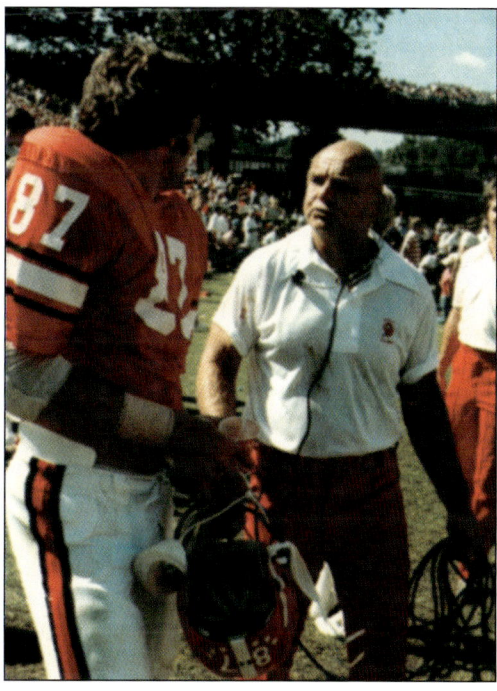

Considered one of the greatest assistant coaches in the history of college football, defensive coordinator Erk Russell gives instructions to defensive end Dicky Clark during Georgia's epic 21-0 victory over Alabama in 1976. The postgame ruckus is regarded as perhaps even more legendary—the so-called "wildest night in the history of Athens" that ensued on Milledge Avenue.

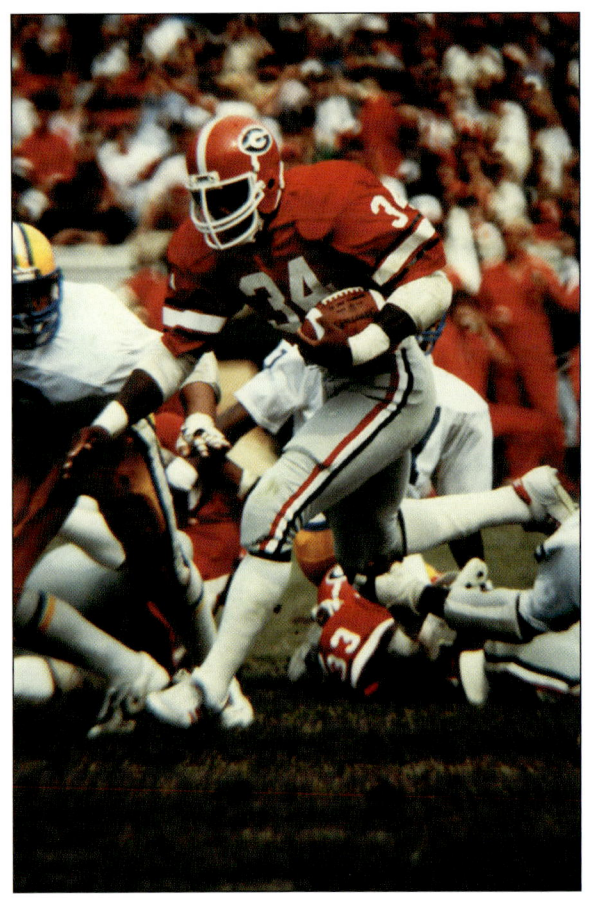

After capturing the Heisman Trophy in 1982 as college football's most outstanding player and leading the Bulldogs to their second national championship game in three years, Herschel Walker left UGA early for the upstart United States Football League. Over the next 30 years, he returned to Athens to open two hamburger restaurants: the health-conscious D'Lites of America in 1984 and Herschel's Famous 34 Pub and Grill in 2013. (Courtesy of Terry Allen.)

As football stadium announcers have declared for decades, "Keep your seats, everyone—the Redcoats are coming!" This 1984 photograph shows UGA's Redcoat Marching Band marching onto the field at Sanford Stadium. By that time, the Redcoats were not only considered one of the largest marching bands in the nation but one of the most entertaining. The Redcoats put on elaborate and impressive halftime shows equaled by few—if any—other college marching bands.

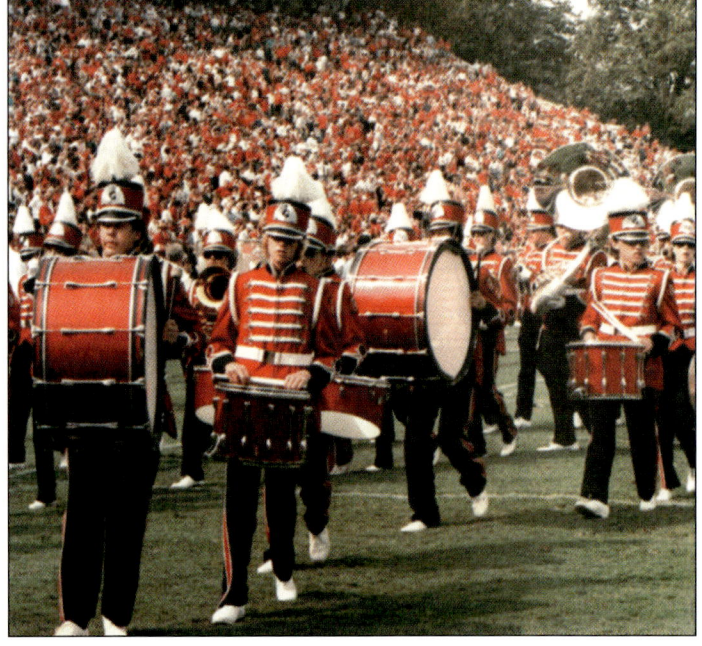

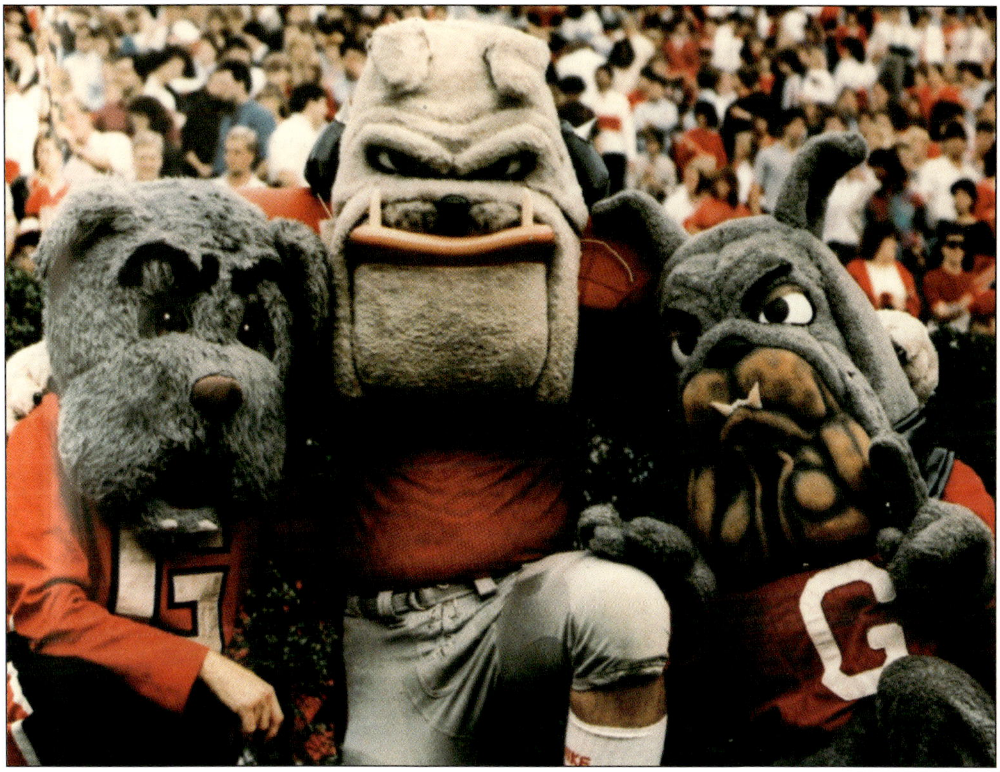

Today, Georgia football fans are accustomed to one costumed mascot, Hairy (center), who was created for the 1981 Sugar Bowl and has been patrolling the Bulldogs' sideline ever since; however, there was a time, including when this photograph was taken in 1985, when UGA football had three "dogs." Before Hairy, there was Fluffie (left), who was created in 1975 by coach Mike Castronis, and Frankie (right), who was created in 1983 and followed Hairy as the third costumed canine.

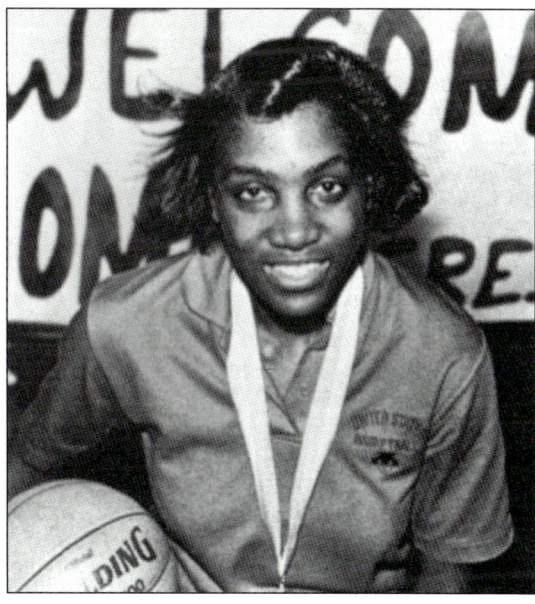

In this image, Georgia women's basketball player Teresa Edwards is welcomed home after winning gold in the 1984 Summer Olympic Games after her sophomore year at UGA. The 1985 and 1986 All-American, who led the Lady Bulldogs to Final Four appearances in 1983 and 1985, is the only male or female basketball player to compete in five Olympic Games for the United States. Edwards also brought home gold medals in 1988, 1996, and 2000, plus a bronze in 1992.

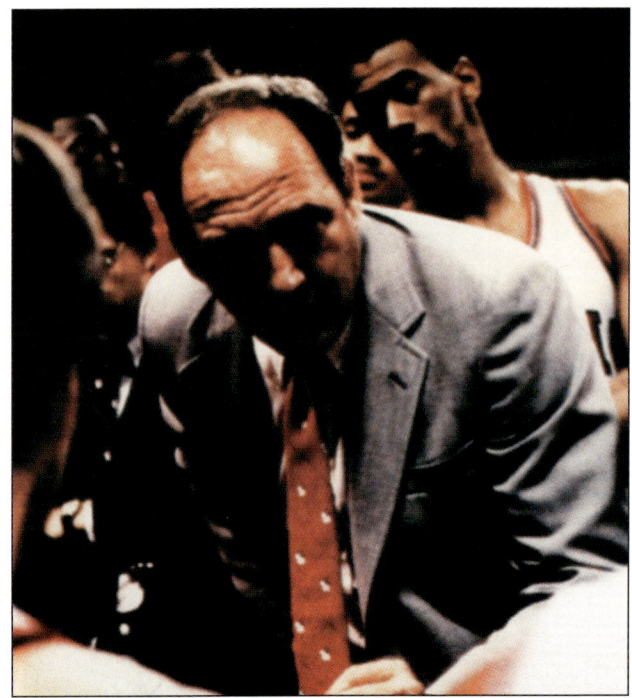

Prior to Hugh Durham's arrival in 1978, the Georgia men's basketball team had endured 23 losing campaigns in its previous 27 seasons of play and had not made any national postseason appearances. Durham, pictured here in 1985, suffered just two losing years in 17 seasons at Georgia, while his teams reached either the NIT or NCAA Tournament on 12 occasions.

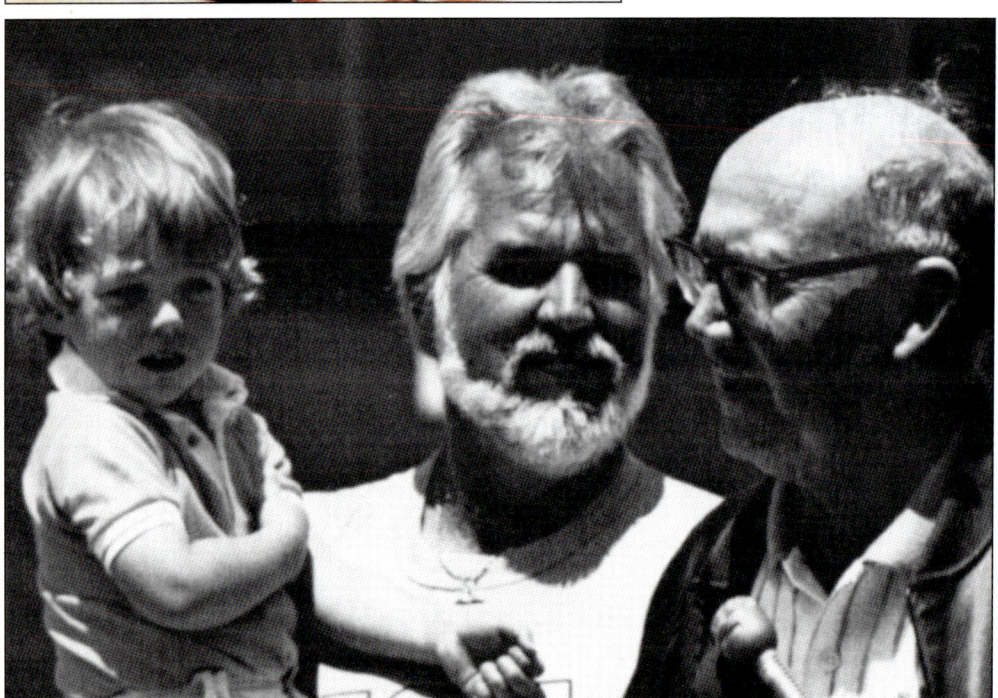

UGA's Dan Magill (right), the all-time winningest men's tennis coach in NCAA Division I history, guided the Bulldogs' tennis team to national championships in 1985 and 1987. Magill is pictured here in 1984 with country music star Kenny Rogers (center) and Rogers's son Christopher (left). Rogers financed moving the Intercollegiate Tennis Association (ITA) Men's Collegiate Tennis Hall of Fame facility to the UGA campus.

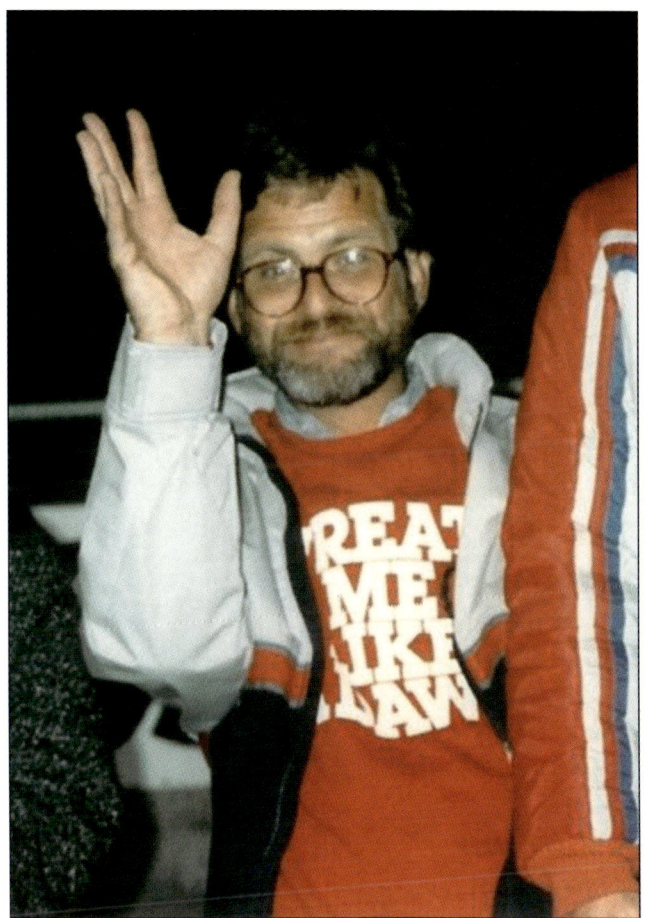

The legendary Lewis Grizzard is pictured at a Georgia football game in 1986; he is sporting a T-shirt that reads, "Treat Me Like A Dawg." Renowned writer and humorist Grizzard attended the University of Georgia during the 1960s, studying journalism and later writing for the independent *Athens Daily News*, shunning the student newspaper *The Red and Black* and rival *Athens Banner-Herald*. Grizzard was an avid Bulldogs fan until his death from complications of heart surgery in 1994. According to his wishes, some of his cremated ashes were scattered at the 50-yard line of Sanford Stadium. (Courtesy of Rob Saye.)

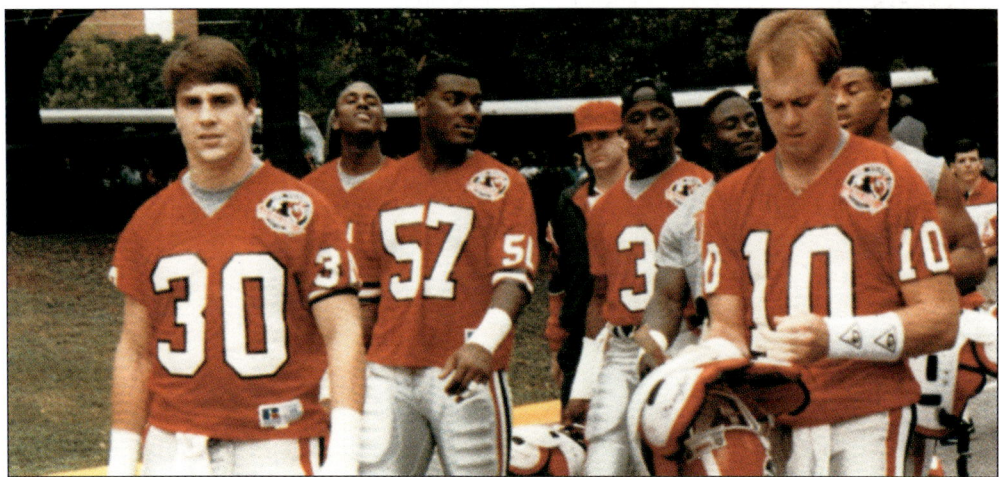

The 1992 Georgia football team, which was celebrating the 100th anniversary of the football program, walks as a group to Sanford Stadium prior to a game against Ole Miss. Notables pictured here include defensive back Will Muschamp (No. 30), assistant coach Joe Tereshinski (center, wearing red cap), quarterback Eric Zeier (No. 10), running back Garrison Hearst (behind Zeier, to the left), and receiver Andre Hastings (behind Zeier, to the right).

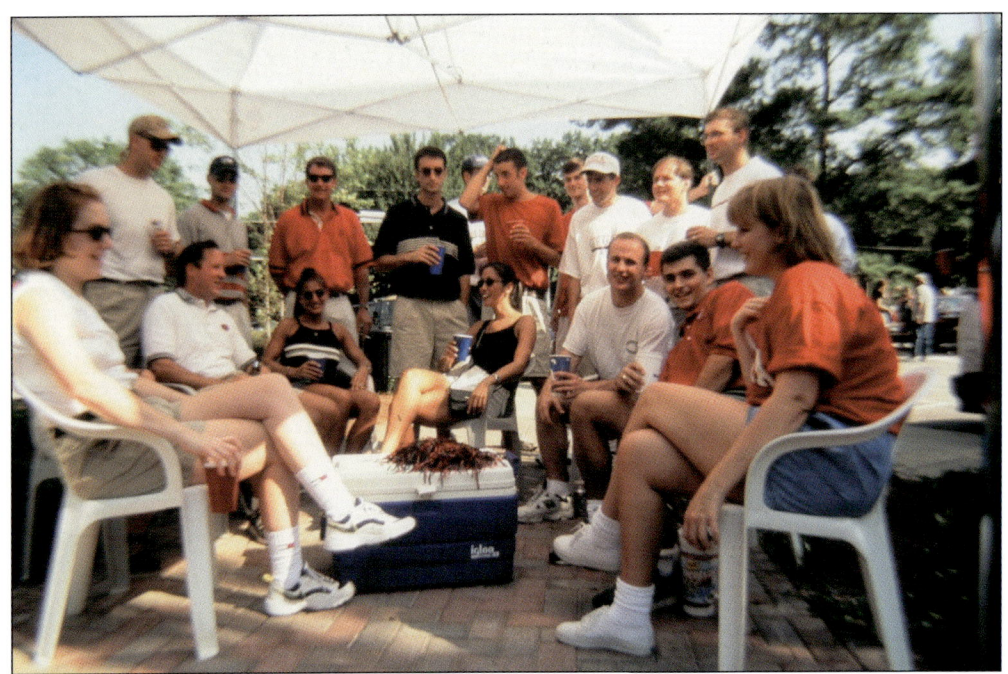

As the size of Sanford Stadium increased during the 1980s and 1990s, the football game-day crowds grew larger, which resulted in more and more tailgaters. This group of tailgaters is pictured prior to a game in the 1990s. Following the 1998 season, the KFC Ultimate Tailgating Search ranked Georgia football's tailgating as the third-best in the nation, just behind Penn State (first) and Michigan (second) and ahead of SEC members LSU (eighth) and Tennessee (ninth). (Courtesy of Terry Allen.)

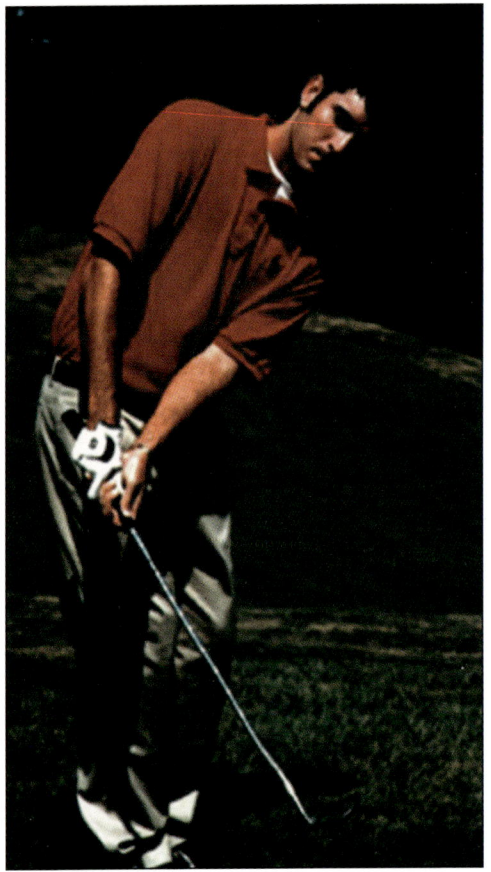

Before he captured the 2012 and 2014 Masters Tournaments, Bubba Watson played for the Bulldogs. Watson was a member of Georgia's 2000 and 2001 men's golf teams, helping the Dogs claim an SEC championship his first year in Athens. Bubba's wife, Angie Ball Watson, is also a Bulldog and lettered on UGA's women's basketball team from 1997 to 2000.

Suzanne Yoculan (right) gives direction to one of her "Gym Dogs" during their national championship season in 1999. Yoculan was the head coach of Georgia's gymnastics team for 26 seasons, from 1984 through 2009. During her tenure, the Gym Dogs remarkably captured 10 national championships, including five in a row in Yoculan's final five seasons (2005–2009).

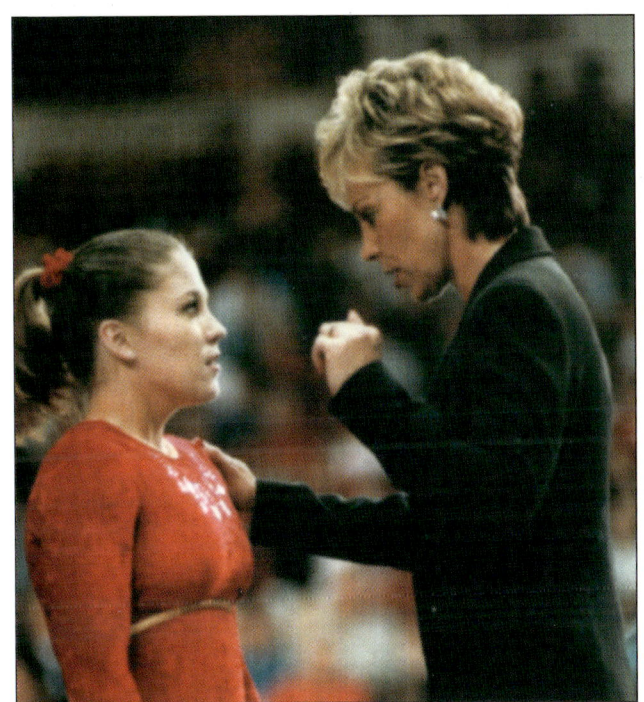

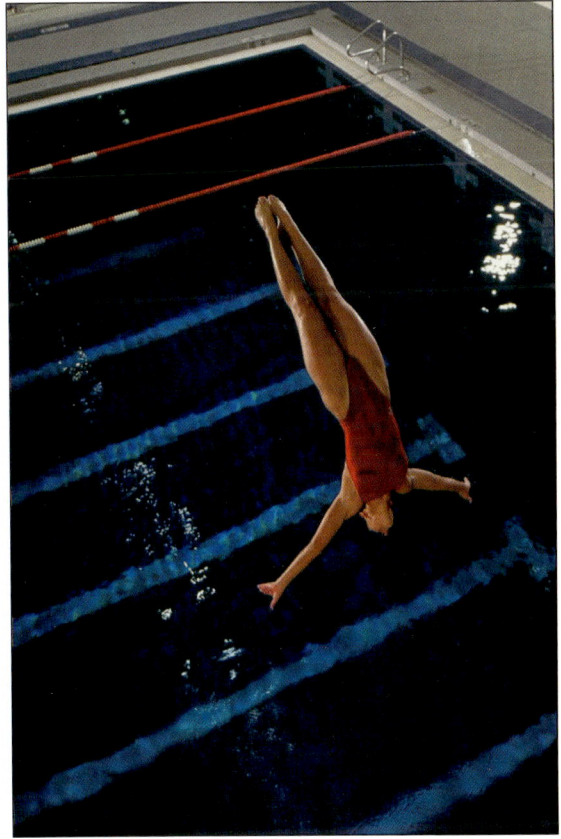

A member of the "Swim Dawgs" takes a dive at UGA's Gabrielsen Natatorium just a few years after the swimming and diving facility opened in the mid-1990s. Soon thereafter, the Georgia women's swimming and diving team won its first of six NCAA national championships in a 16-year span: 1999, 2000, 2001, 2005, 2013, and 2014. (Courtesy of Terry Allen.)

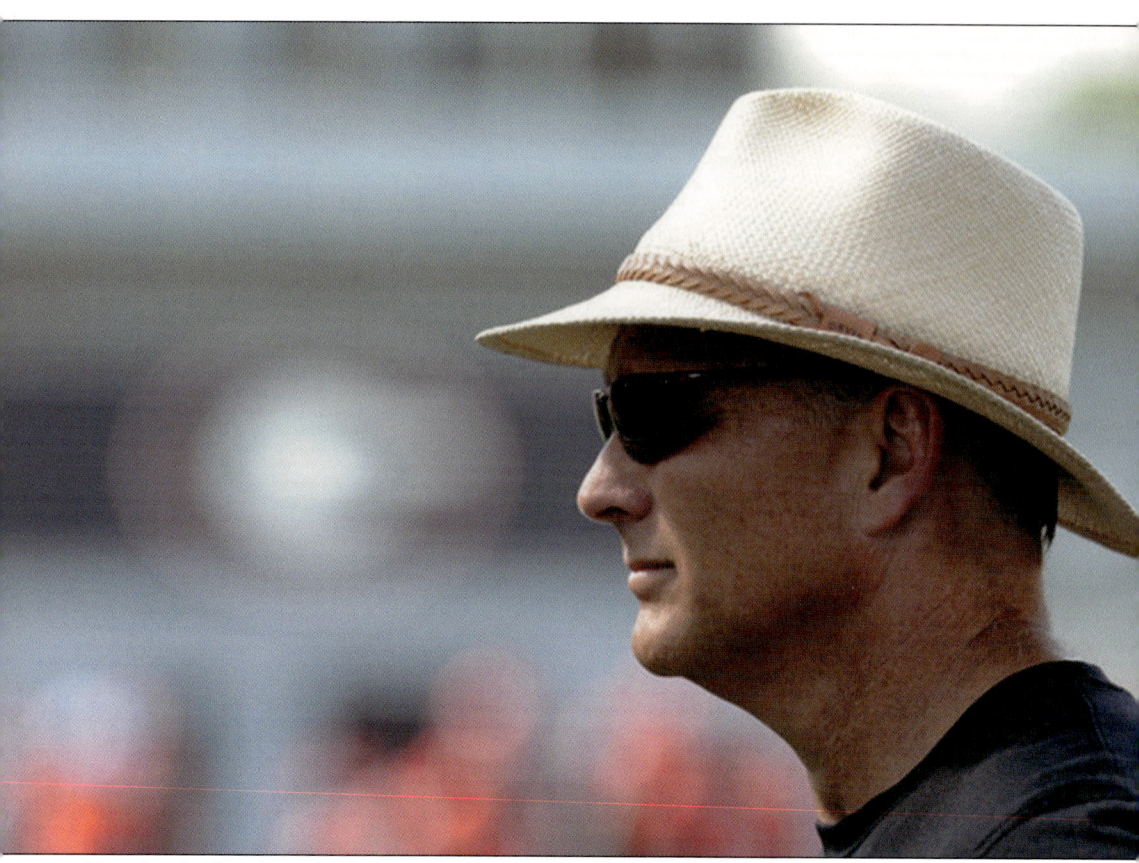

Shortly after head coach Mark Richt's arrival in Athens in 2001, the UGA football team achieved a level of success the program had not experienced in some time. Richt guided the Bulldogs to SEC championships in 2002 and 2005, top-10 final national rankings in four consecutive seasons (2002–2005), and a no. 2 final ranking in 2007. (Courtesy of McGinnis Leathers.)

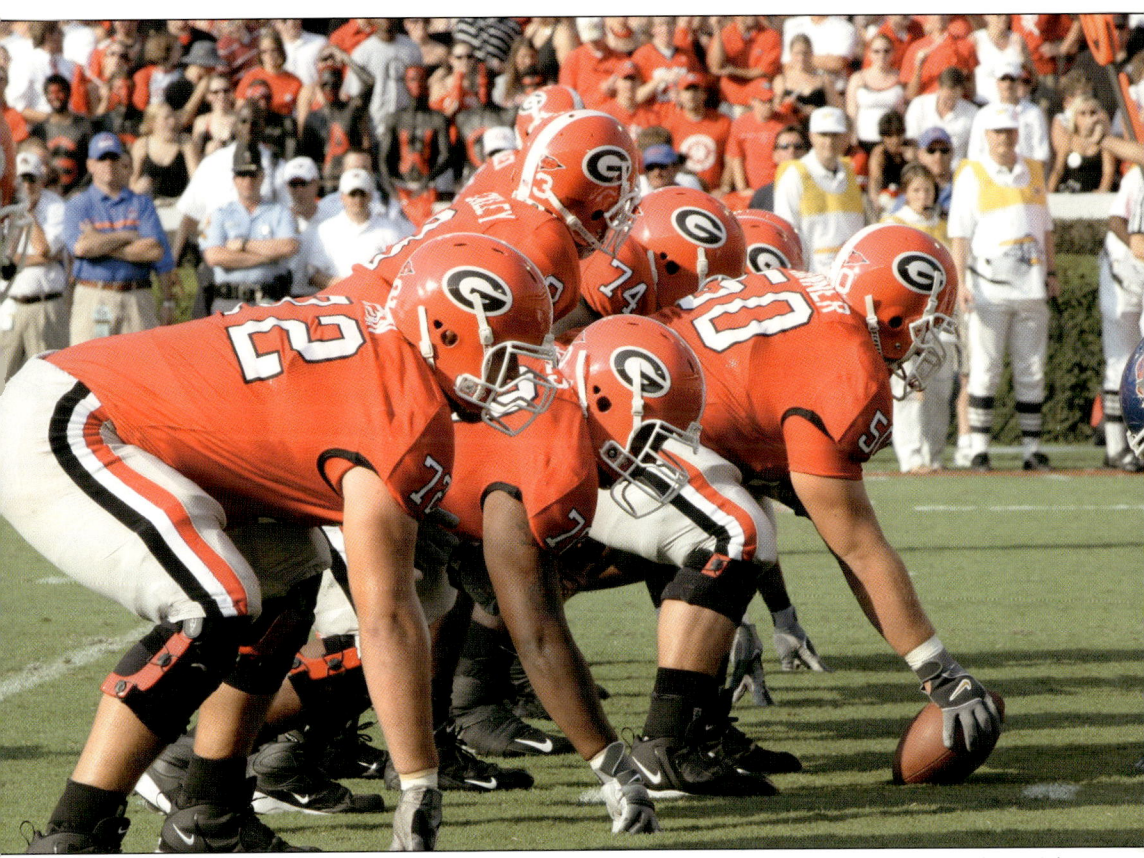

Quarterback DJ Shockley (No. 3) is set to receive the snap from center Russ Tanner (No. 50) during Georgia's 2005 season opener against Boise State. In the Bulldogs' 48-13 rout of the Broncos, Shockley set a single-game school record by being responsible for six touchdowns. The victory was Georgia's first in what would eventually result in 10 wins for the season and an SEC championship. (Courtesy of Jerry Howell.)

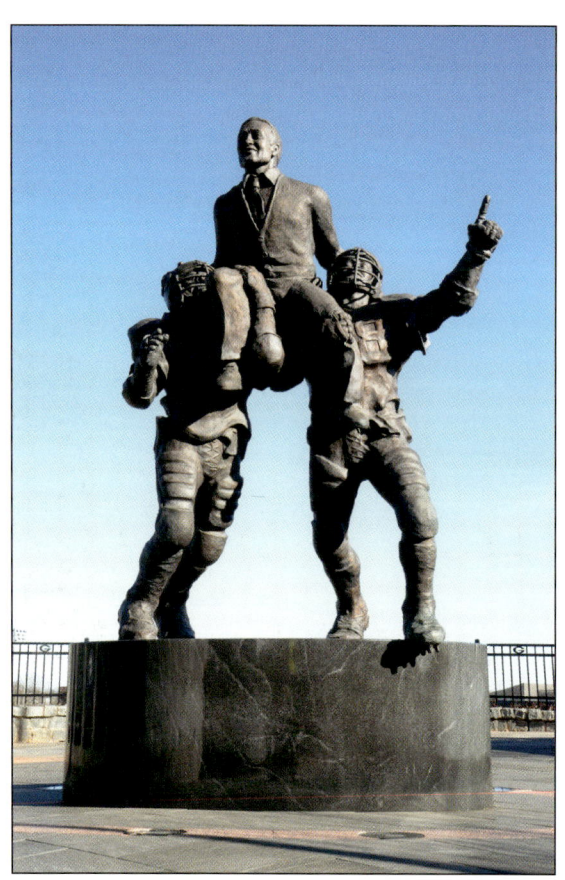

Almost 20 years to the day after Vince Dooley registered his 200th career victory in his final season as Georgia's head football coach in 1988, a statue of him was unveiled in November 2008 in a new garden area constructed next to the UGA track and the Butts-Mehre Heritage Hall. The statue depicts the moment when Dooley was given a victory ride by linemen Tim Morrison and Jeff Harper after the Bulldogs defeated Georgia Tech in 1980. (Courtesy of McGinnis Leathers.)

In 2008, shortly after his final broadcast as Georgia football's acclaimed radio play-by-play man—a position he filled for more than 40 years—Larry Munson salutes and waves goodbye to a sellout crowd at Sanford Stadium. The "Voice of the Bulldogs" will always be regarded as one of the greatest sports announcers of all time, while all UGA announcers who came before or will follow are considered secondary to legendary Larry.

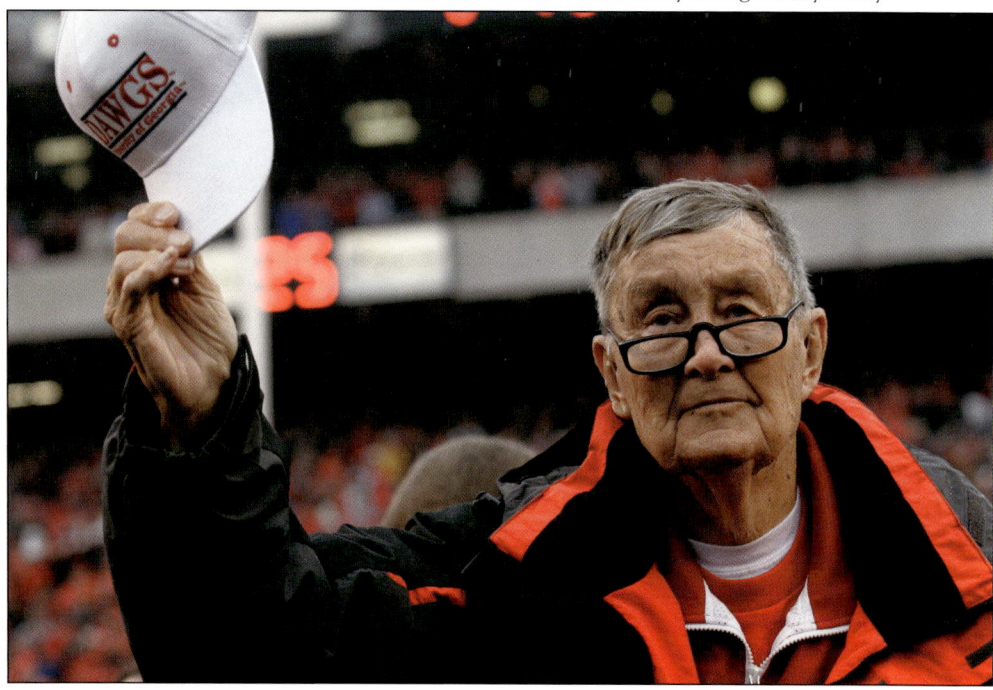

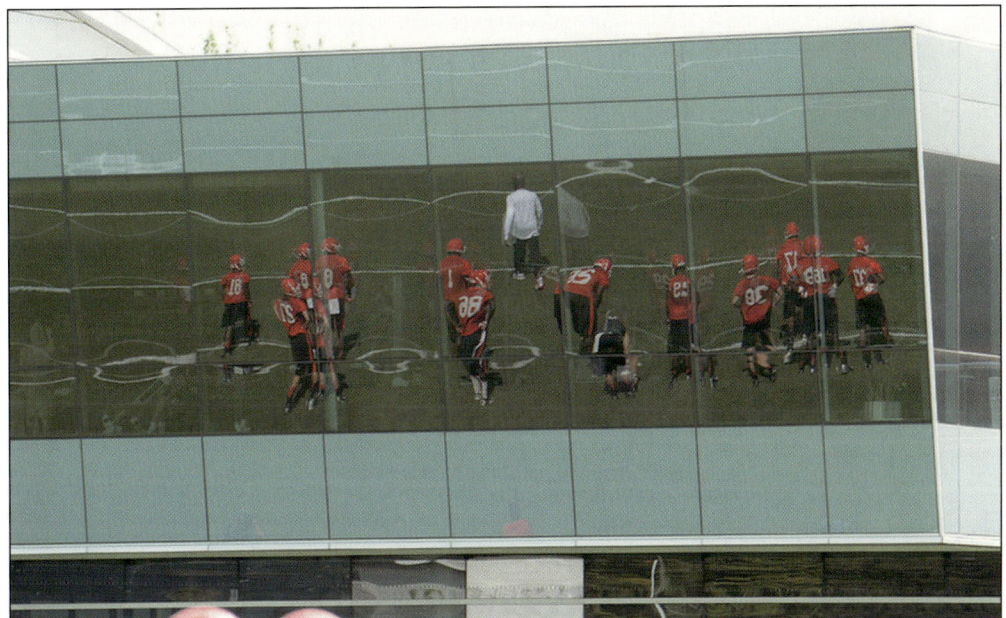

Georgia football players preparing for the start of the 2011 season are reflected in the glass of the upgraded Butts-Mehre Heritage Hall. The building, which was originally dedicated in 1987, had a $33-million makeover in February 2011, which included 53,000 square feet of new space and 23,000 square feet of renovated space. (Courtesy of McGinnis Leathers.)

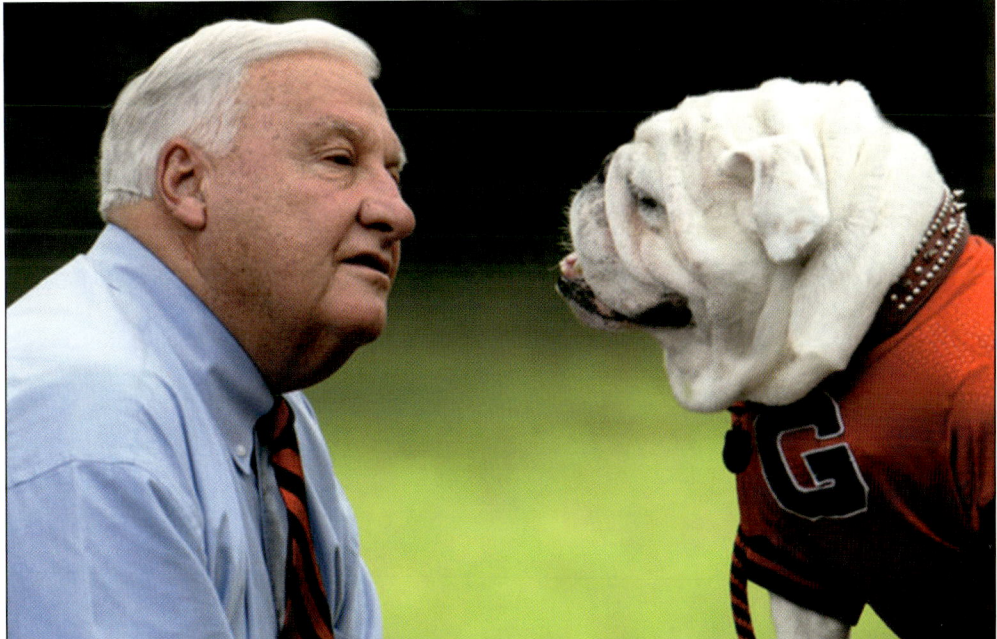

Beginning in 1956, a live English bulldog—fittingly named "Uga" (pronounced "ugh-ah")—has represented the University of Georgia as the school's official mascot. To date, there have been nine Ugas, all owned by Sonny Seiler (pictured) of Savannah. Notably, there have been a handful of bulldog replacements to fill in for Uga when duty called, including Bugga Lou, Knute, Otto, and Magillicuddy I. The latest replacement, Russ, eventually became Uga IX. (Courtesy of Terry Allen.)

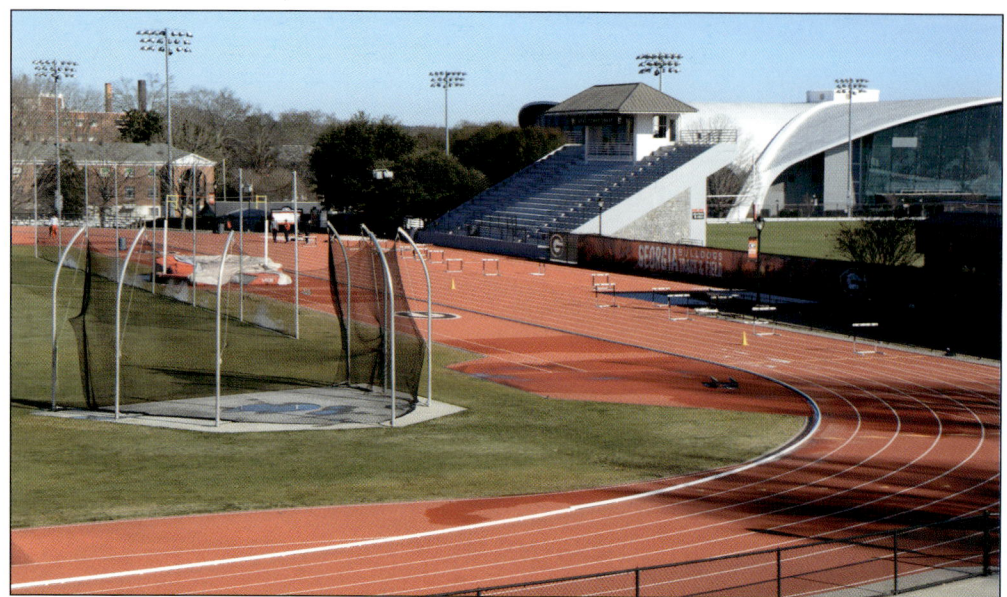

Shortly after the opening of the Coliseum (right background), the UGA track was built nearby in 1964. The track's grandstand, which was added in 1987, can accommodate roughly 1,000 spectators. Officially named the Spec Towns Track in 1990 for legendary UGA track coach and 1936 Olympic gold medalist Forrest "Spec" Towns, the facility hosted the SEC Outdoor Track & Field Championships in 2011 for the first time in a dozen years. (Courtesy of McGinnis Leathers.)

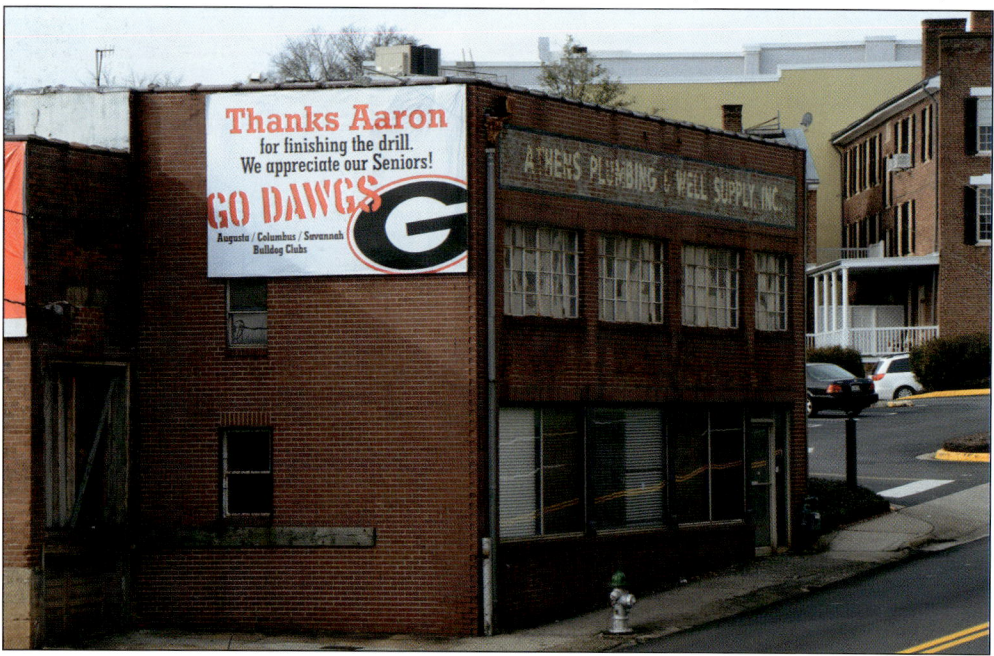

Prior to the 2013 football season, a few Bulldog Clubs in the state erected a "Thanks Aaron" sign on the side of the downtown Athens Plumbing & Well Supply building. Along with the Bulldogs' other senior players, the clubs were recognizing Aaron Murray—arguably the greatest quarterback in the history of Georgia football—for returning for his final season at UGA instead of entering the NFL draft. (Courtesy of McGinnis Leathers.)

Five
THE MUSIC SCENE AND CULTURE

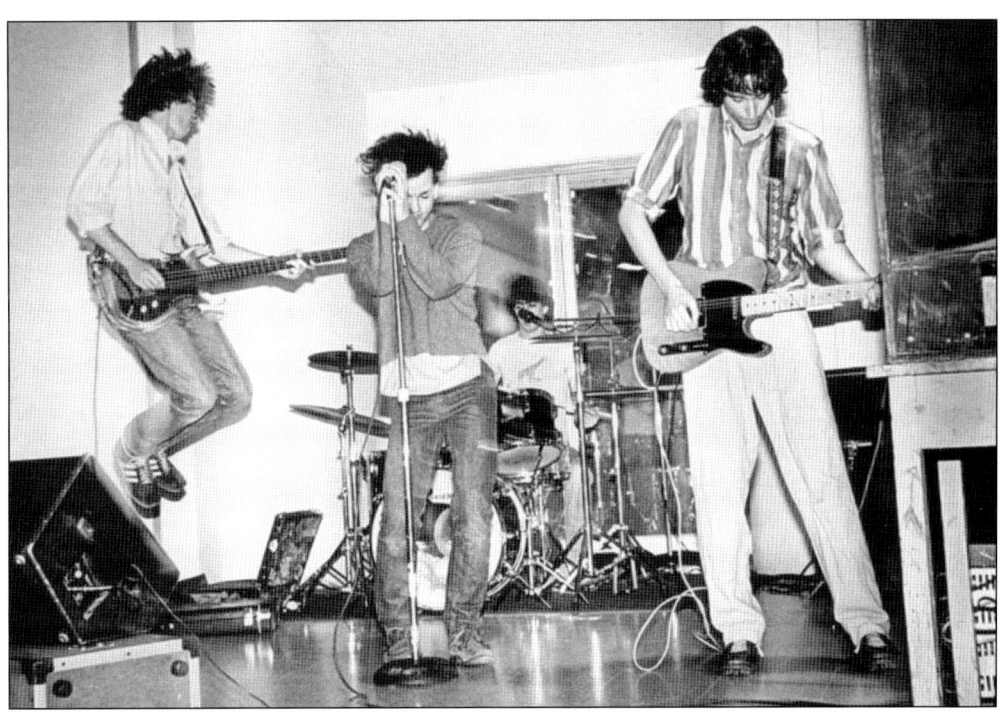

From left to right, Mike Mills, Michael Stipe, Bill Berry (on drums), and Peter Buck—who collectively made up R.E.M.—perform at the UGA Art Department in 1980. Stipe had been an art major, studying painting and photography, at UGA. The band used this photograph for the cover of the 2006 album, *And I Feel Fine . . . The Best of the I.R.S. Years 1982–1987*. (Courtesy of Terry Allen.)

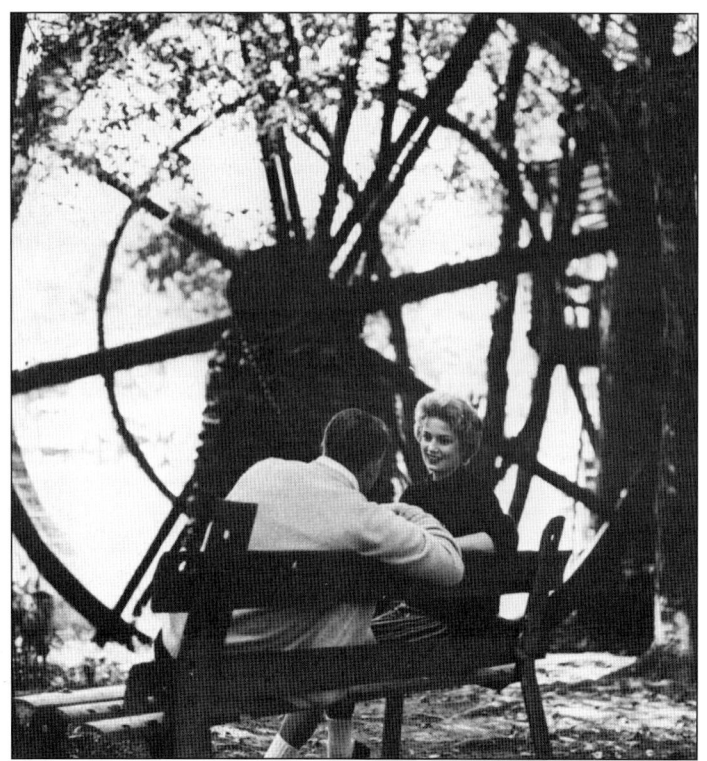

During the 1960s, Athens's top bands—like the Jesters, Zodiacs, and Blue Blenders, to name a few—could mostly be found playing at fraternity houses and a place like Charlie Williams Pinecrest Lodge. Charlie Williams, which featured the distinguished waterwheel shown in the background of this image, was a happening place to dance to some great bands or just enjoy a fine meal.

Soon after UGA's Coliseum opened in 1964, it began hosting musical acts, including the great Ray Charles, who played there in October 1966. After hundreds of hopeful spectators were turned away at the Coliseum's doors, it was reported that Charles "delighted a capacity crowd of over 10,000 University and townspeople for three echoing hours."

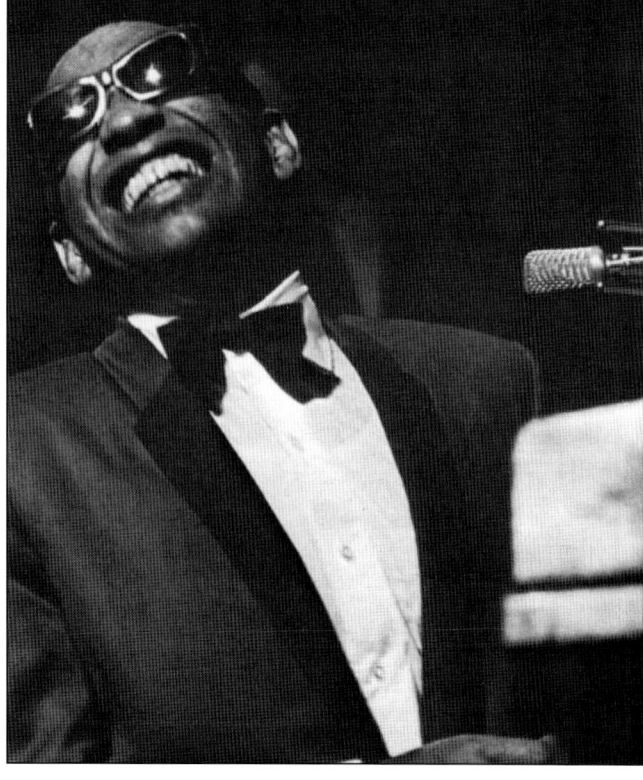

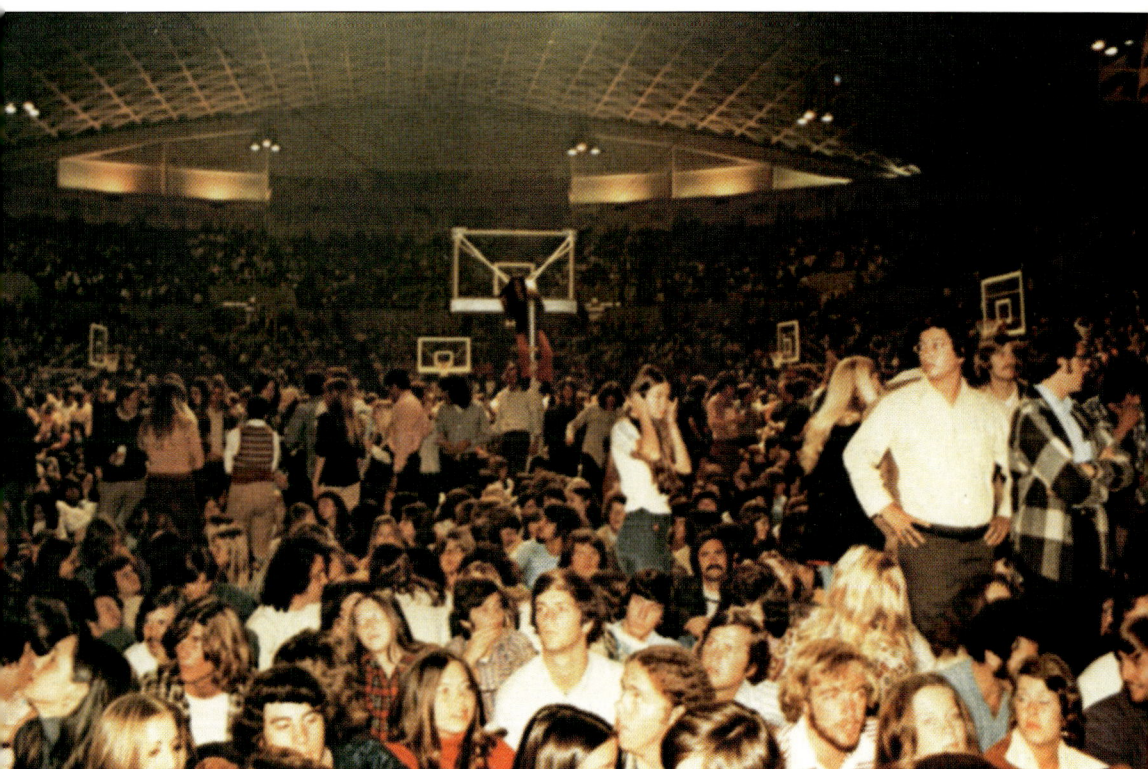

This photograph shows concertgoers on the floor of the Georgia Coliseum prior to the start of the January 19, 1973, concert by the Allman Brothers Band—the only time the legendary band has played in Athens. It was estimated that of the 11,718 spectators in attendance, roughly 2,000 were seated on the floor, where "abuse of alcohol and marijuana" took place, leaving the floor "a detestable mess" and prompting the state fire marshal to limit Coliseum floor seating to 760.

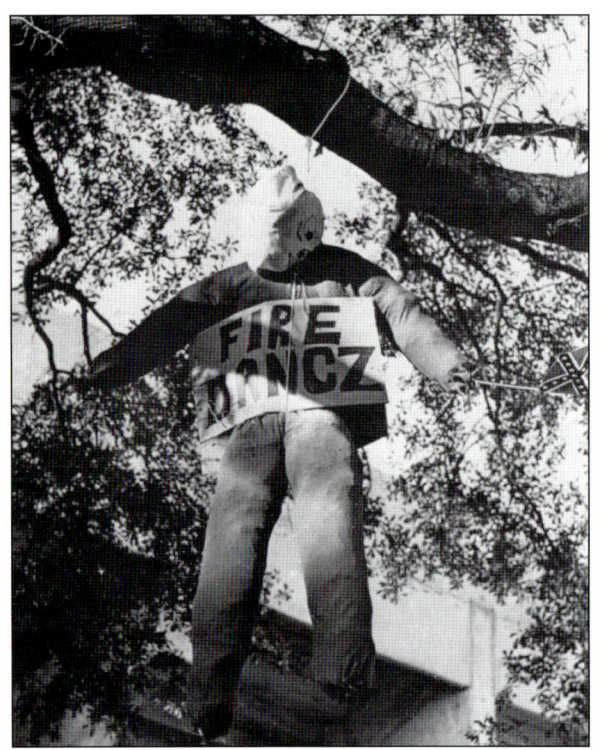

After UGA Redcoat Band director Roger Dancz dropped the song "Dixie" from the band's performance schedule in 1971, the backlash he fielded came from many individuals and lasted for several years. Even in 1974, when UGA students voted overwhelmingly in favor of the Redcoats having the song return to their repertoire, Dancz held his "no Dixie" stance. The backlash became outrageously nasty, as shown by this hanging effigy of Dancz. Note the Confederate flag in the dummy's hand.

The University Union has brought some of the greatest musical acts of the 20th century to Athens. In October 1976, the union sponsored Jackson Browne and his opening act, Orleans, at the Georgia Coliseum. Browne's 10-song performance, which lasted for 70 minutes, was described as "powerful." Browne commented during his show, "I didn't even know Athens was here, but I'm glad I know now."

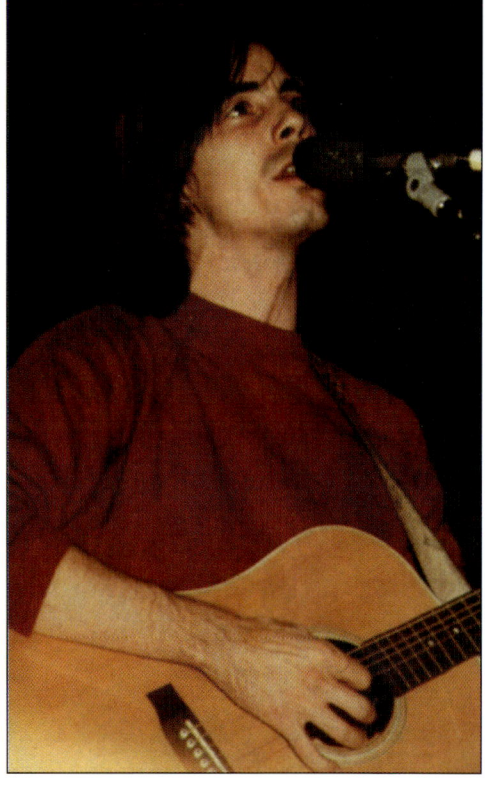

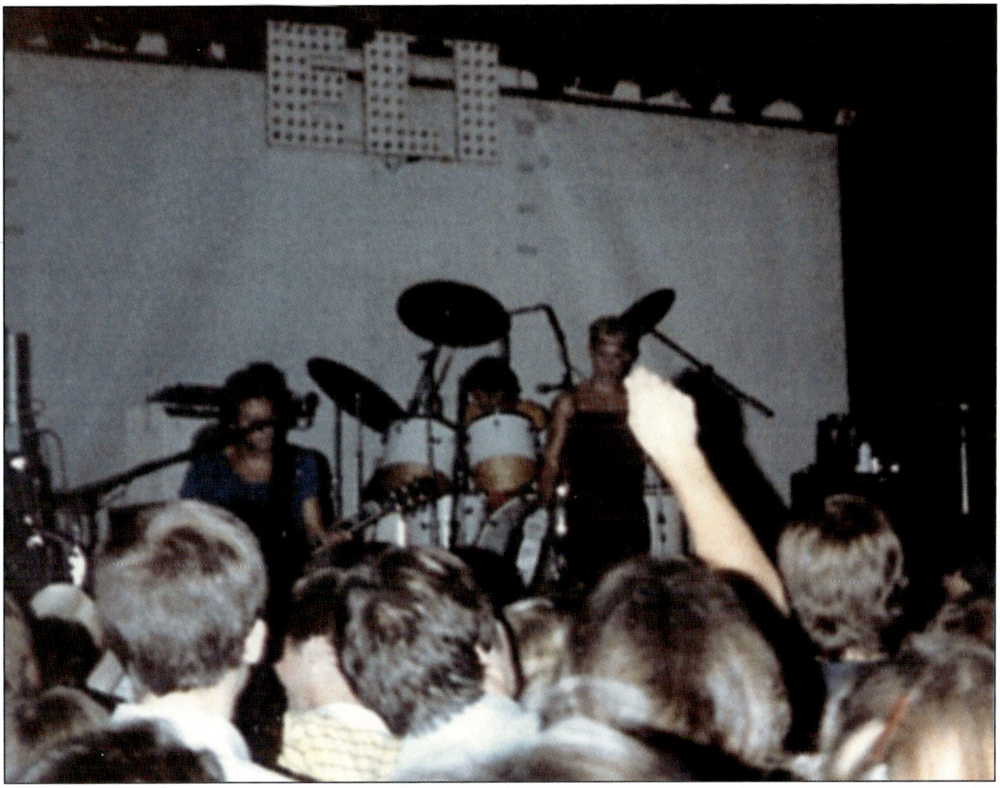

Whether at a fraternity band party, the B&L Warehouse, or the Mad Hatter, ELI attracted a crowd from the mid-1970s to the mid-1980s. The band played covers of KISS, Led Zeppelin, Peter Frampton, ZZ Top, and what was described as "an incredible Beatles medley." The lead singer of ELI, Dale Cook, was better known by his nickname, "Cookie." (Courtesy of Rob Saye.)

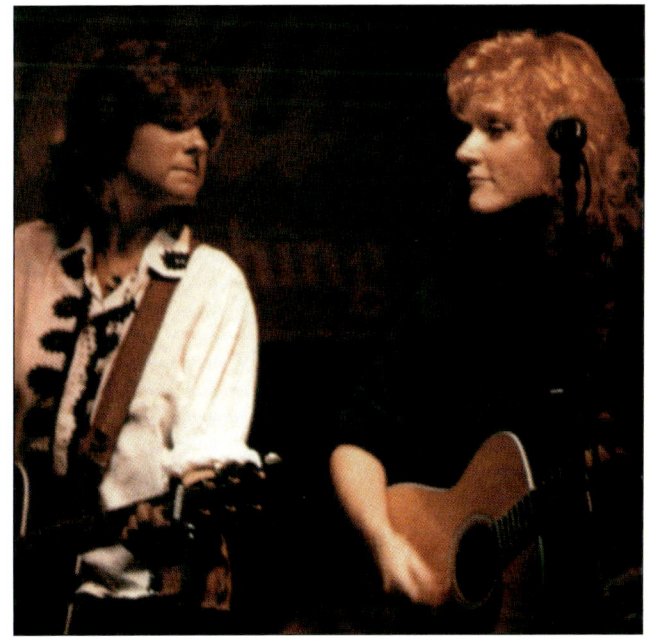

Although the Indigo Girls—Amy Ray (left) and Emily Saliers (right)—are originally from Atlanta, they are tangentially considered part of Athens's celebrated rock scene. This photograph of the Indigo Girls was taken in the late 1980s, shortly after the release of their first full-length album, *Strange Fire*, which was recorded at John Keane Studios in Athens.

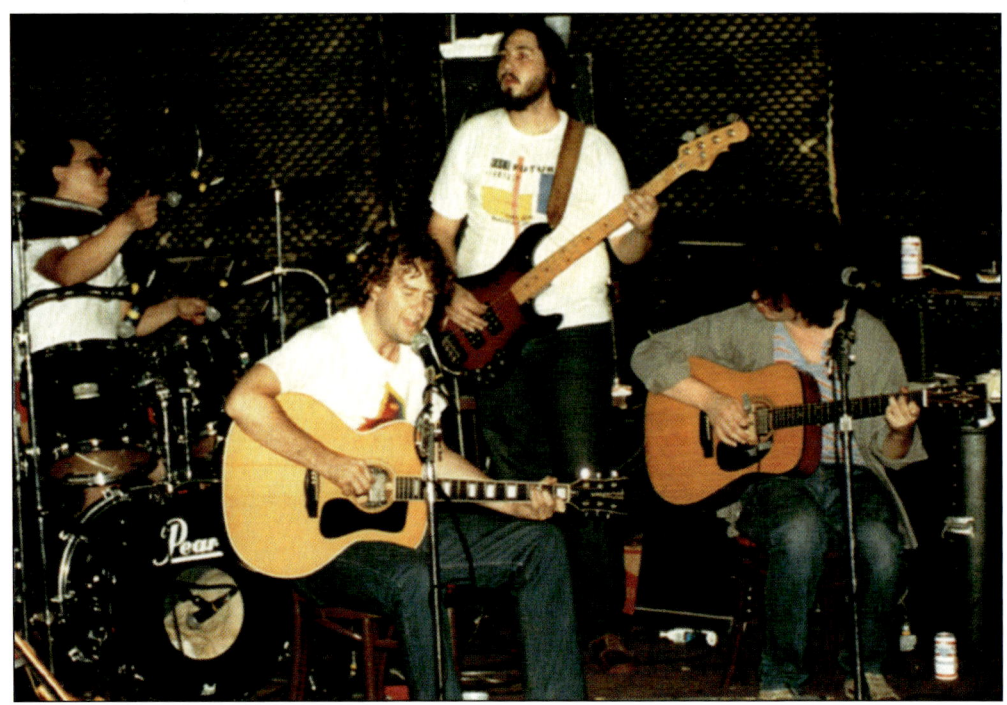

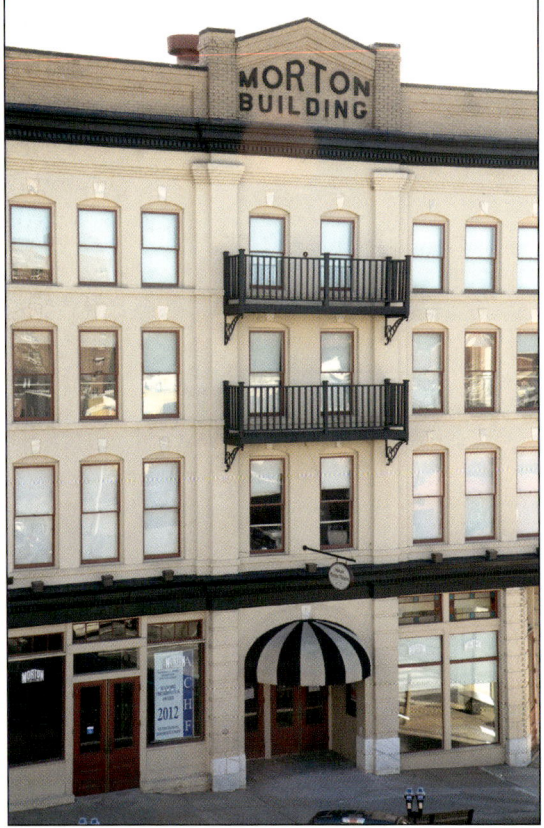

Before they became household names, UGA students John Bell (center, sitting), Dave Schools (center, standing), and Michael Houser (right) helped form the band Widespread Panic in the 1980s. After the band made its first appearance on February 24, 1985, at the "A-Frame house" on the corner of Weymanda Circle and Weymanda Court in Athens, and before reaching stardom, they performed at the city's U.S. Aware '85 festival and several times at the Uptown Lounge in downtown Athens.

Established in 1910, the Morton Theatre remains one of the first and oldest surviving vaudeville theaters in the United States built, owned, and operated by African Americans. During the 1980s, after the theater portion of the building had gone unused for decades, the Morton Theatre was purchased using a combination of state and federal funds and then renovated with county funding. (Courtesy of McGinnis Leathers.)

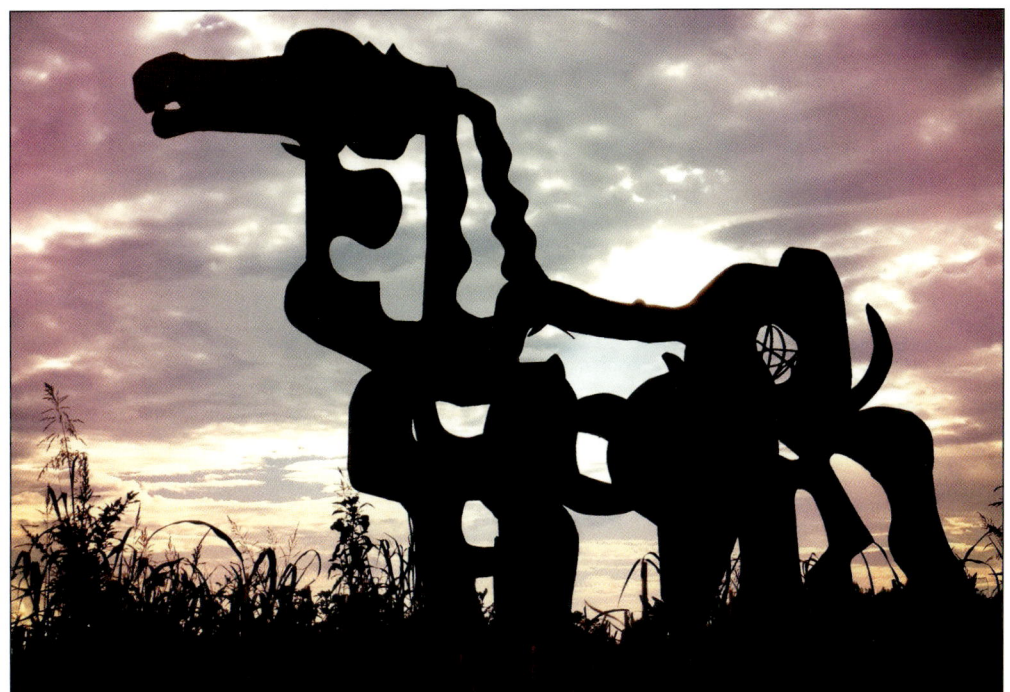

In May 1954, the 12-foot-tall, one-ton Iron Horse stood on the UGA campus for less than 24 hours. After it was vandalized by students, the sculpture was promptly moved to a secret location. Today, it stands 18 miles from Athens in a Greene County cornfield off Georgia Highway 15. In 1982, a movement led by the president of the Interfraternity Council, Steve Fiveash, was initiated to bring the horse back to campus, but to no avail. (Courtesy of McGinnis Leathers.)

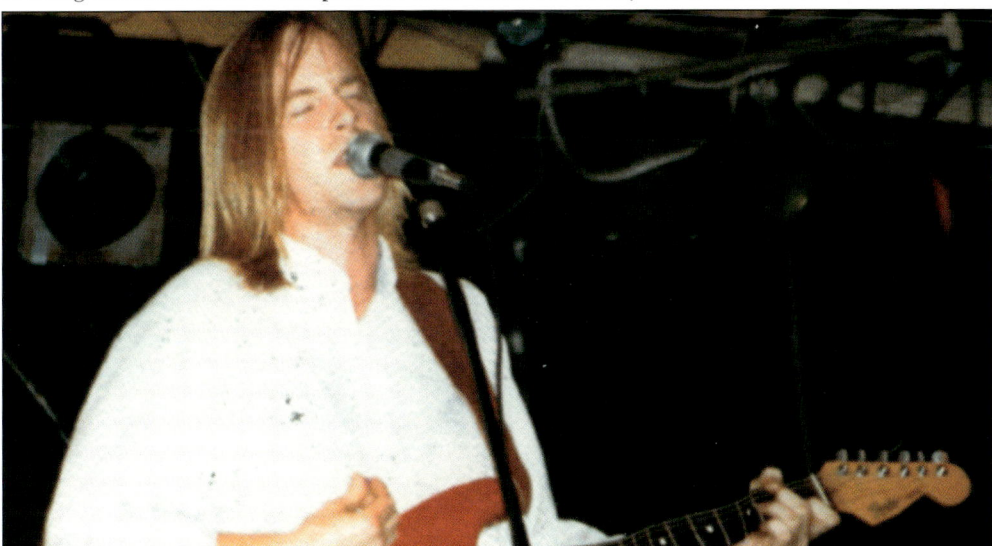

Michael Winger of Dayroom is pictured performing in Athens in the early 1990s. A staple in the city's music scene during the 1990s, the rock band once estimated that it performed 200 times per year, often in Athens, and regularly at the Georgia Theatre. Dayroom, a band recognized by Lisa Perron of the *Atlanta Music Examiner* as "the greatest band you've never heard," performed for the final time in October 2001 at the Georgia Theatre.

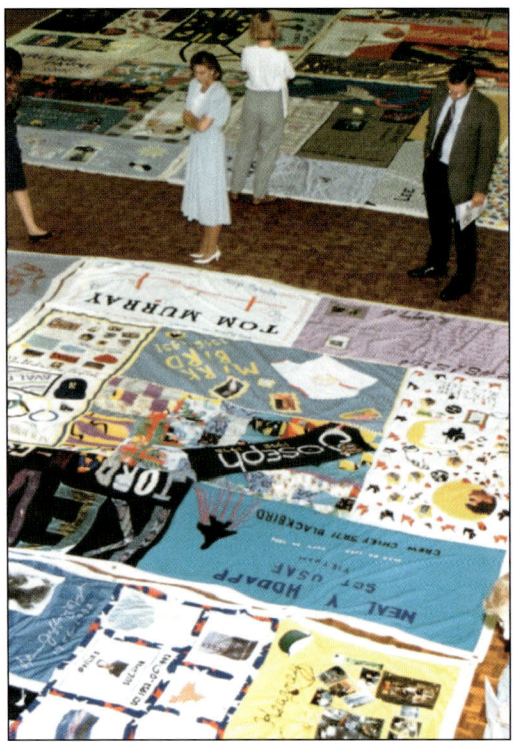

This image is from 1995, when the AIDS Memorial Quilt came to UGA's Tate Student Center. The quilt was created in 1987, and this was the third time it came to Athens, having previously been displayed in 1991 and 1992. In 2013, the quilt was displayed for three days at Athens's Classic Center.

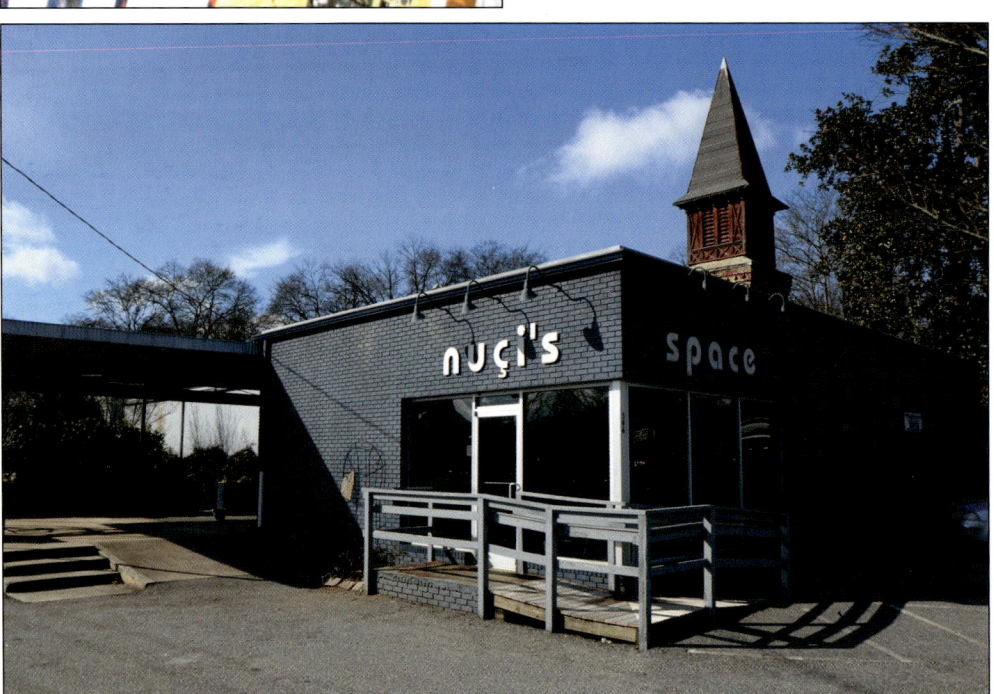

Andre Nuçi Phillips was a 22-year-old UGA student and guitarist for local band Koncak before he died on Thanksgiving Day in 1996. In his memory, Nuçi's Space was formally dedicated in October 1998. Linda Phillips, Nuçi's mother, created the spot for musicians to rehearse, get counseling, and "just be musicians." (Courtesy of McGinnis Leathers.)

"Boybutante"—a drag ball—was organized in Athens in 1989. Five friends who founded Boybutante are recognized not only for starting the drag movement in the community, but also for assisting in the city's gay movement. Going to a drag show or gay-friendly event in Athens was once improbable; however, by the 1990s, the city had plenty to offer the gay community.

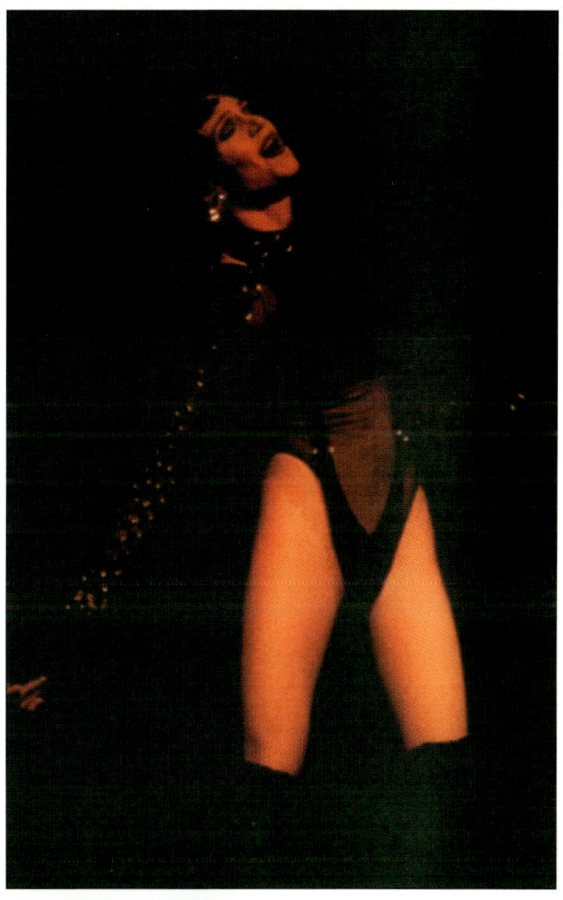

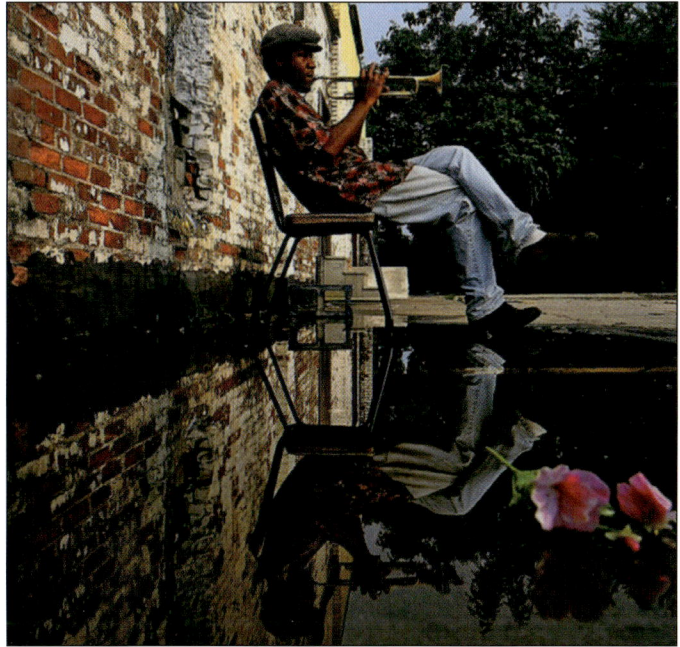

Vernon Thornsberry is pictured here playing his trumpet outside his Washington Street art studio in the late 1990s. Thornsberry is originally from New Orleans, but after visiting Athens on vacation in 1986, he decided to call the Classic City his new home. A "narrative artist," Thornsberry can often be spotted riding his bike between the Jittery Joe's on East Broad Street and The Grit on Prince Avenue. (Courtesy of Terry Allen.)

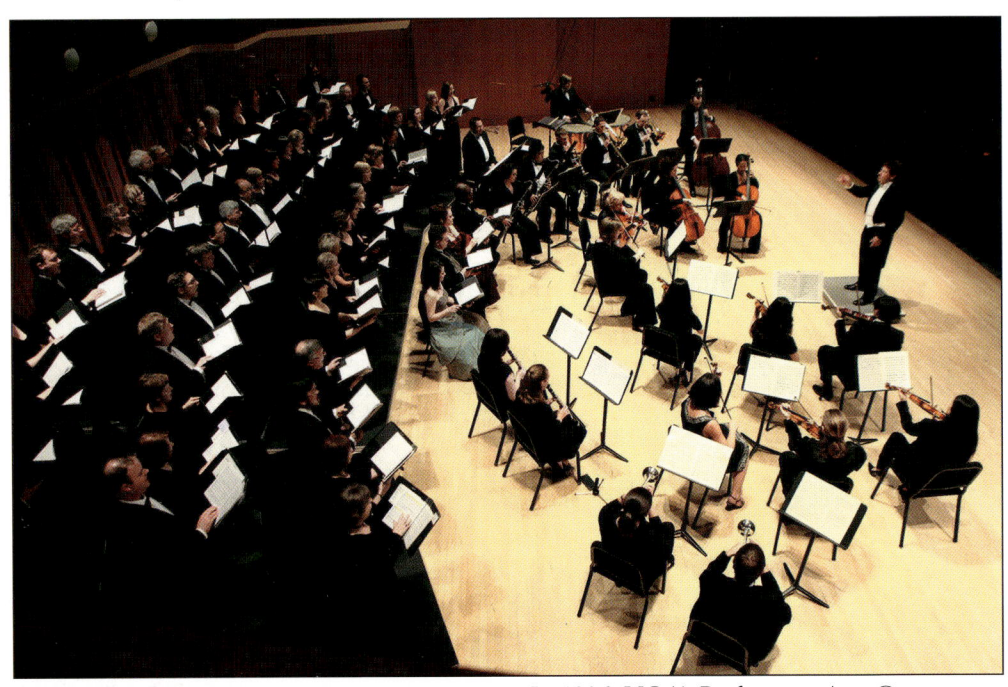

In 1996, UGA's Performing Arts Center opened on River Road and, according to the *Atlanta Journal-Constitution*, began "changing the way the university spends its days and nights." Instantly, the best acts from around the world began performing in Athens, including renowned symphony orchestras, well-known opera singers, jazz legends, and reputable ballet troupes. (Courtesy of Terry Allen.)

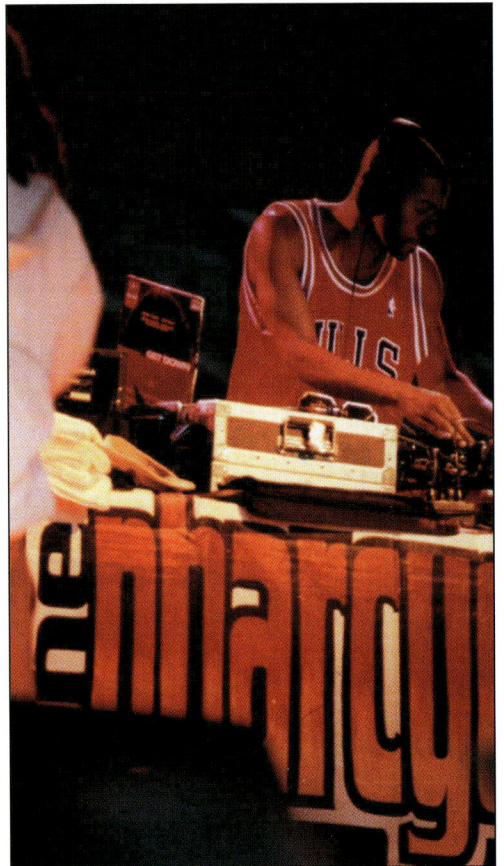

For most of the 1990s and into the 2000s, UGA's CBCP (Committee for Black Cultural Programs) or the University Union sponsored the "Day of Soul," a celebration of African American culture that included a concert performed at Legion Field. The May 1996 concert (pictured) was headlined by hip-hop group The Pharcyde.

B-52's lead singer Kate Pierson is pictured performing at Stegeman Coliseum for UGA's Homecoming in 1997. After the band formed in 1976, "the Bs" soon made it big, leaving Athens two years after their first gig. "We never really played Athens much after we left," Keith Strickland, guitarist for the new wave band, said just prior to the 1997 Homecoming show, "and it was always something I've regretted."

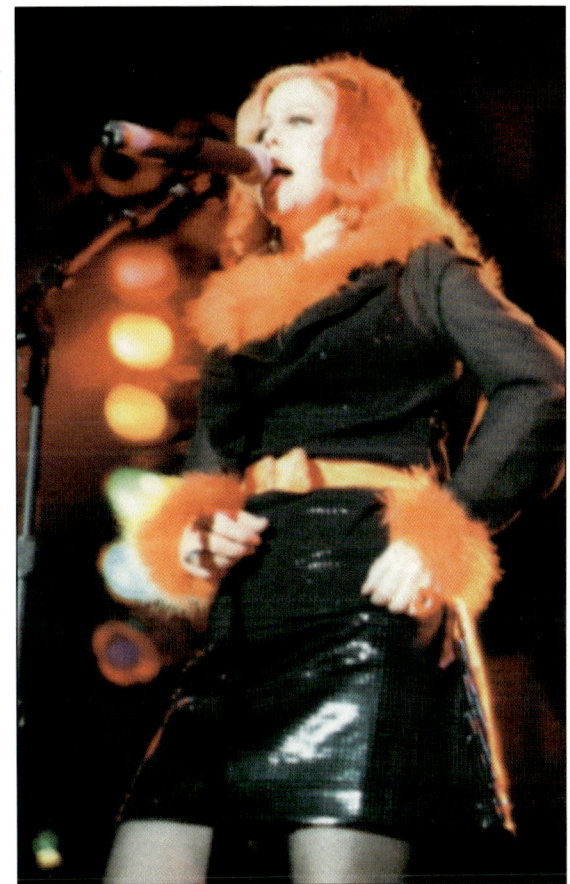

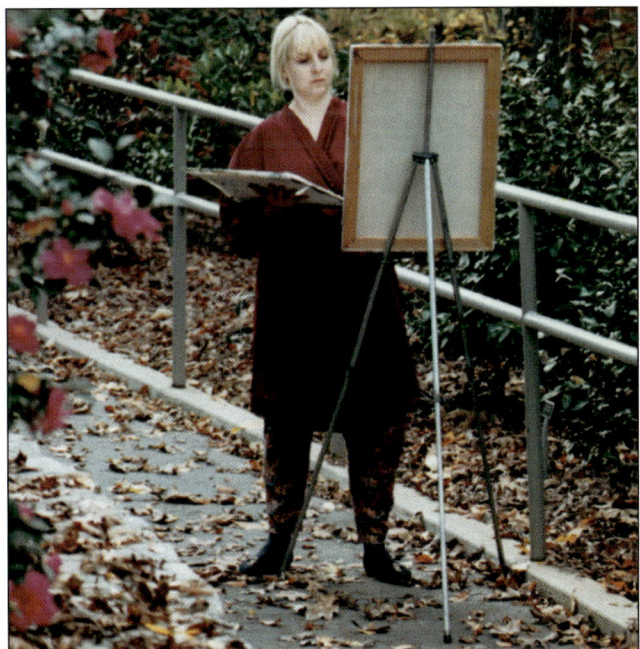

In the late 1990s, an artist captures the beauty of the State Botanical Garden of Georgia located on South Milledge Avenue. More than 20 years prior, Gov. Jimmy Carter had given money from an emergency fund to help plan and develop a "major botanical garden" in Athens for the state of Georgia. Today, the garden covers over 300 acres, equipped with a conservatory operated by UGA, and contains roughly five miles of nature trails.

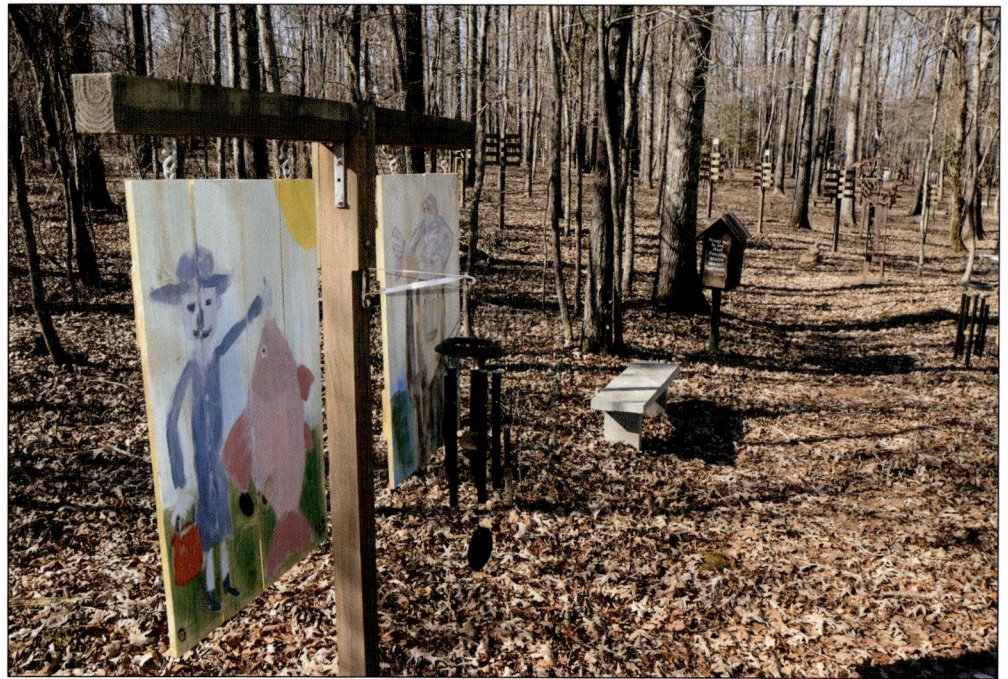

In the wake of the 9/11 tragedy, UGA professor Bob Hart and his wife, Nancy, visited New York City in October 2001. The visit prompted Hart to build a memorial for the 9/11 victims on the Harts' Morton Farm Lane property in Athens. The 9/11 Memorial Trail was completed in six months; it remains a work in progress more than a dozen years later and is open to the public. (Courtesy of McGinnis Leathers.)

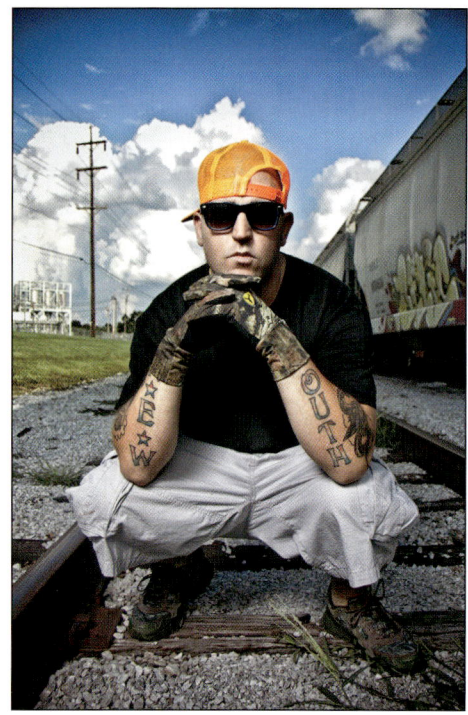

In October 2001, Georgia-bred rapper Bubba Sparxxx had an album release party for his first album, *Dark Days, Bright Nights*, at the downtown Athens club Gator Haters. Partygoers included a who's who of hip-hop: OutKast, Goodie Mob, and Timbaland. The album's song "Ugly," which climbed as high as No. 15 on the Billboard Hot 100, was partially filmed at the Walmart Lexington on the east side of Athens. (Courtesy of Average Joes Entertainment.)

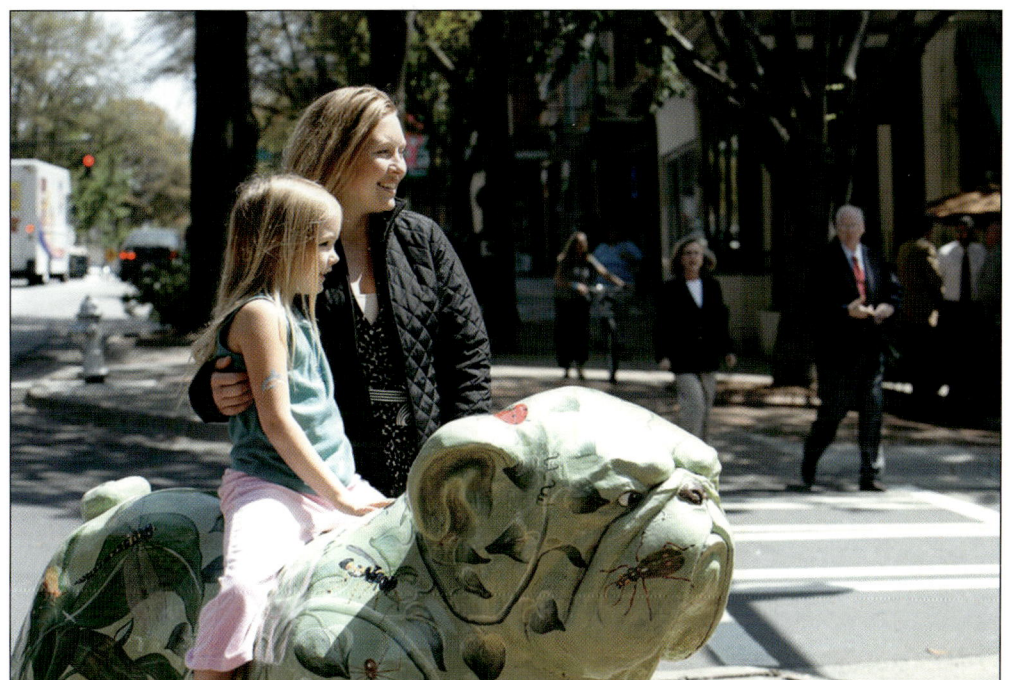

In 2002, a total of 38 three-foot-tall bulldogs were placed in the downtown, Normaltown, and Five Points areas of Athens. The "We Let the Dogs Out" program, supported by the Athens-Oconee Junior Woman's Club, sold sponsorships—$2,500 per bulldog—to local businesses and patrons, while selected artists were paid $250 each to paint the bulldogs. (Courtesy of Terry Allen.)

The famous 40 Watt Club's current location on West Washington Street is in a building that housed one of the first grocery stores in downtown Athens and was later used as overflow storage for the Potters House. Pictured on the 40 Watt stage is saxophonist Joe Maneri performing at the club in April 2004.

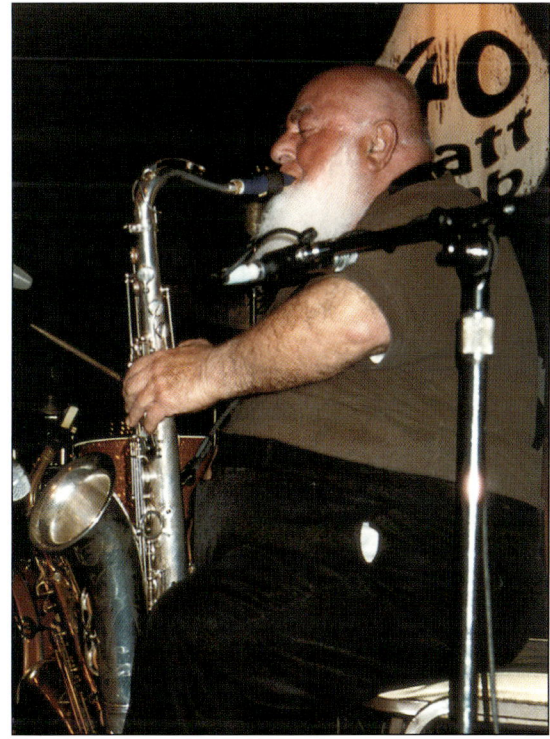

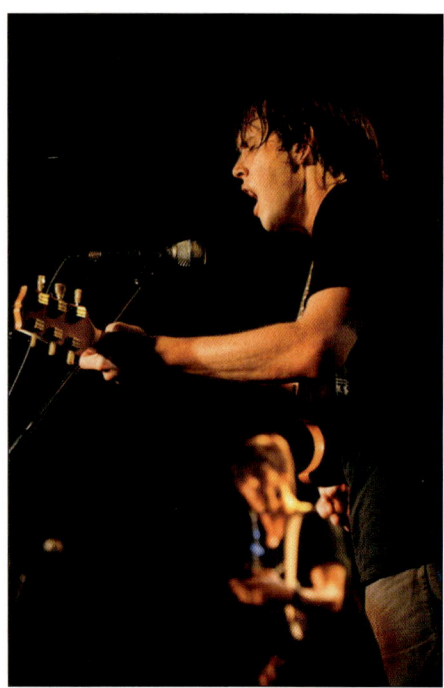

In this mid-2000s image, lead singer Parker Gispert and the rest of The Whigs—Hank Sullivant and Julian Dorio (not pictured)—perform at the 40 Watt Club. Gispert and Dorio are UGA graduates. Sullivant left the band in 2006 and was replaced by Timothy Deaux. The Whigs's third album, *In the Dark*, was recorded in 2009 at Chase Park Transduction studio in Athens. (Courtesy of Terry Allen.)

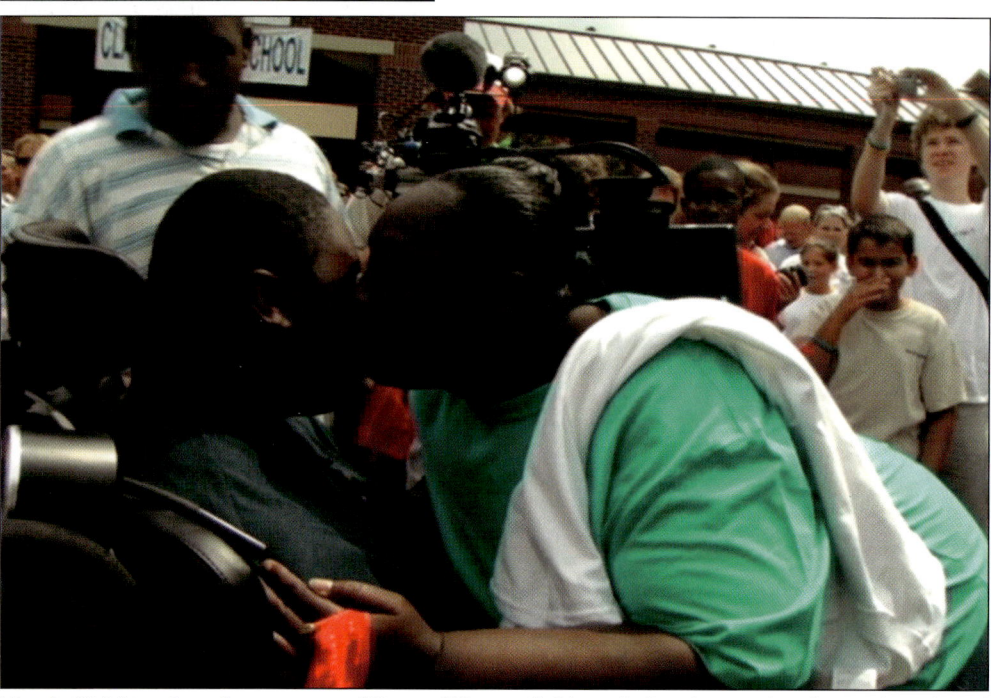

Nearly 200 friends and supporters of Darius Weems (left), including his mother (center), gathered at Athens's Clarke Middle School in 2005 to welcome him home. Weems, a teenager living with Duchenne muscular dystrophy, embarked on a road trip across the country to raise awareness of the fatal disease. The documentary film *Darius Goes West: The Roll of His Life* was released in 2007 and chronicles the Athens–to–Los Angeles trip Weems made along with 11 of his friends. (Courtesy of DariusGoesWest.org, photograph by Dylan Wilson.)

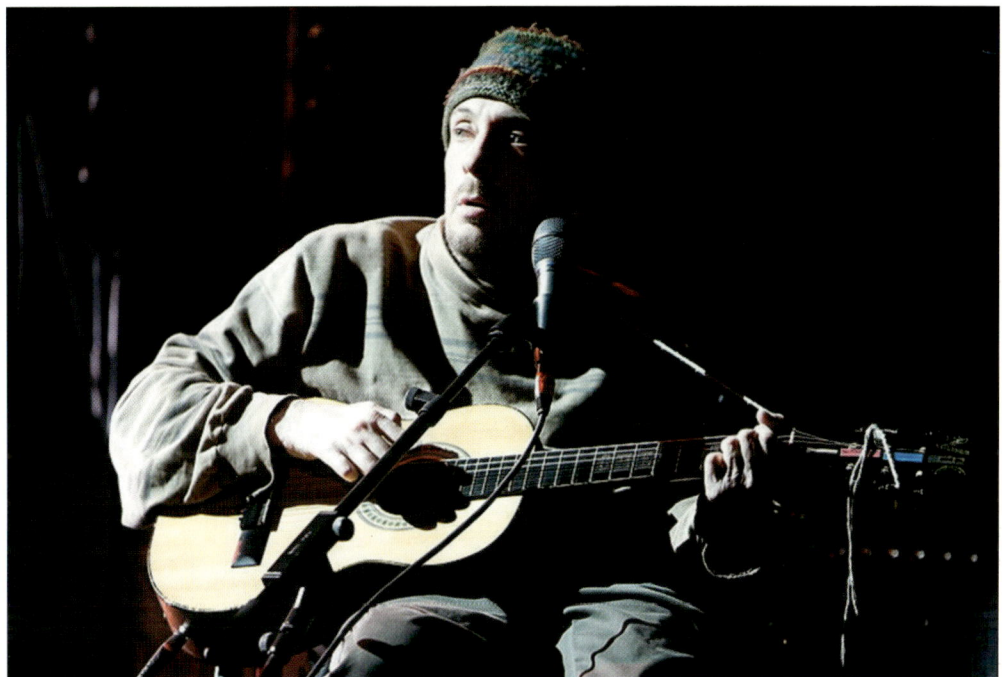

Quadriplegic singer-songwriter Vic Chesnutt moved to Athens during the mid-1980s. He released 17 albums in less than 20 years, including two produced by Michael Stipe. Chesnutt often performed at the 40 Watt Club and is pictured here in 2008; he died on Christmas Day in 2009.

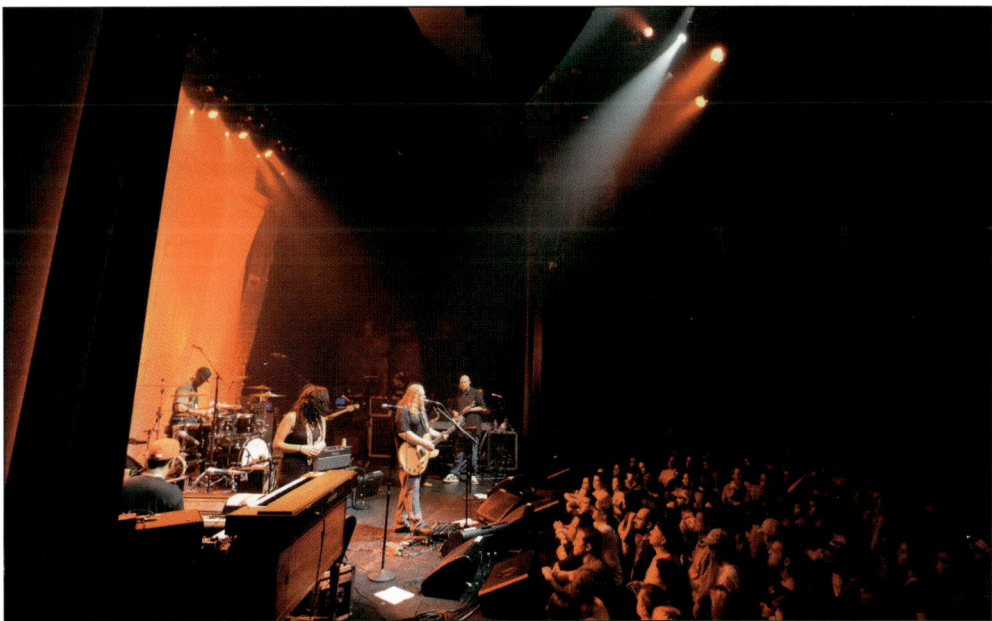

After being closed for more than two years following a devastating fire in 2009, the newly renovated Georgia Theatre reopened on August 1, 2011. The new theater is a concert venue with a state-of-the-art sound system and numerous acoustic improvements along with improved seating, two balconies, and an open-air roof area with a full bar and comfortable patio seating. (Courtesy of McGinnis Leathers.)

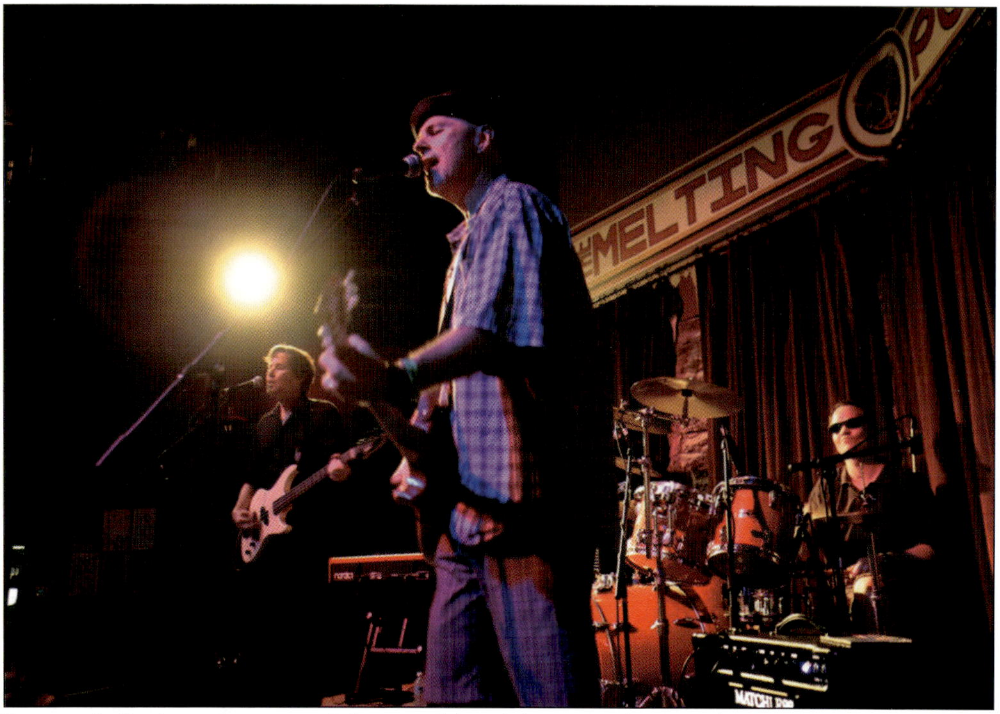

Dreams So Real, an alternative Athens rock band that gained national exposure in the late 1980s and early 1990s, reunited for AthFest in 2009 after nearly two decades apart. Here, the band performs at The Melting Point in April 2012. (Courtesy of Terry Allen.)

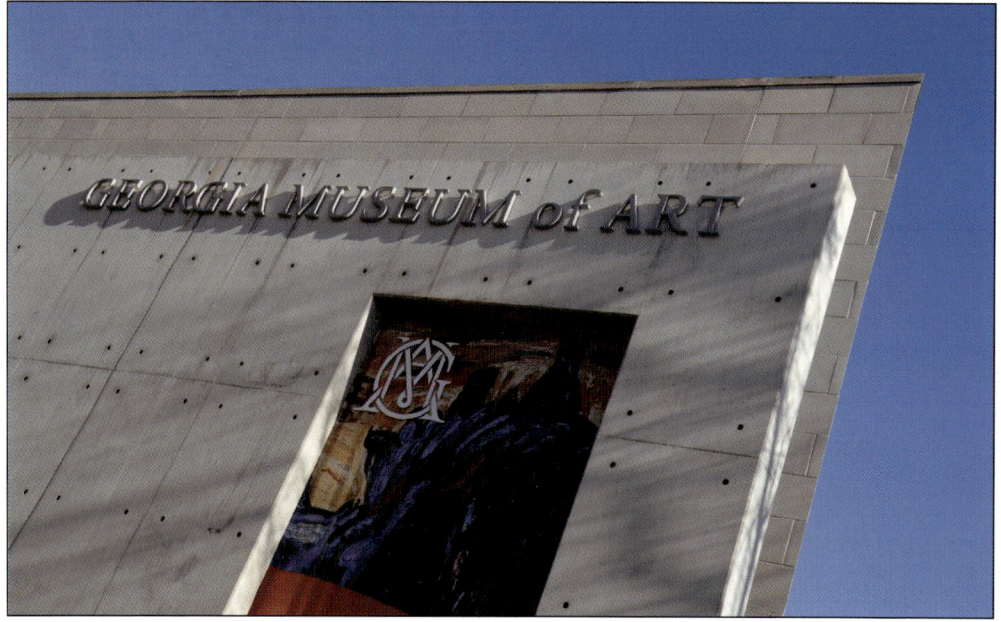

The Georgia Museum of Art opened on UGA's North Campus in 1948 before moving to the Performing and Visual Arts Complex on East Campus in 1996. In 1982, it became the official museum of art for the state of Georgia. In January 2011, the museum opened a new wing alongside the newly renovated existing facility. (Courtesy of McGinnis Leathers.)

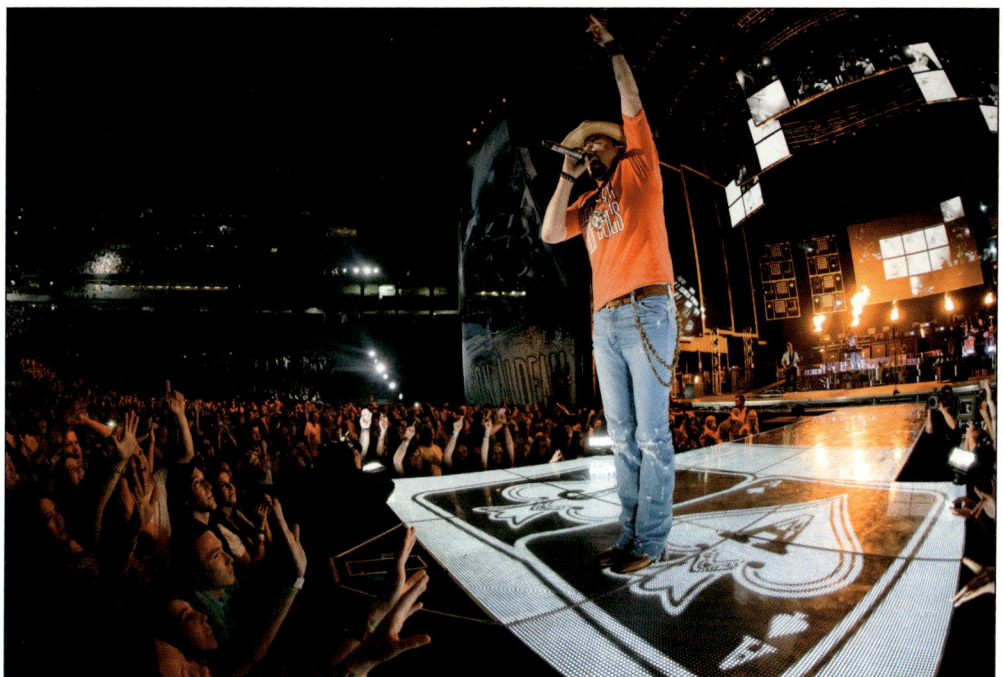

Along with supporting acts Luke Bryan, Jake Owen, and Thomas Rhett, Jason Aldean played at Sanford Stadium on April 13, 2013. The country music star was also joined on stage by rapper Ludacris in a surprise appearance. Aldean called the show "one of the defining moments of my career," and the event, which drew more than 60,000 spectators, was the first concert ever held at the stadium. (Courtesy of Spalding Entertainment, photograph by Todd and Chris Owyoung.)

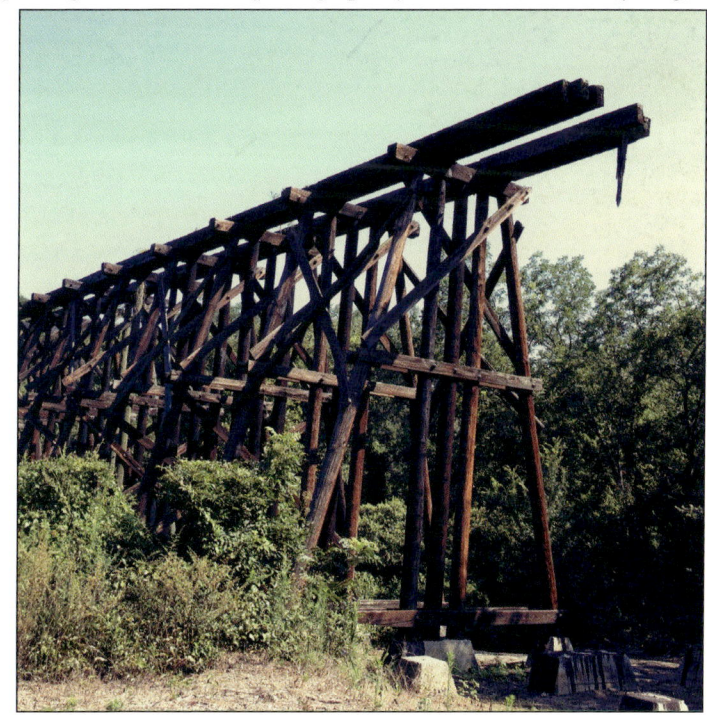

Built in the 1880s as part of the Athens branch of the Georgia Railroad, this partially demolished railroad trestle graced the back cover of R.E.M.'s first full-length album, Murmur, before it was abandoned as a working rail bridge in 1984. Although the trestle was saved from demolition in 2000, funding has not been found to repair it. Alas, as of 2014, it was the apparent near end of the "R.E.M. trestle" as we know it. (Courtesy of McGinnis Leathers.)

Discover Thousands of Local History Books
Featuring Millions of Vintage Images

Arcadia Publishing, the leading local history publisher in the United States, is committed to making history accessible and meaningful through publishing books that celebrate and preserve the heritage of America's people and places.

Find more books like this at
www.arcadiapublishing.com

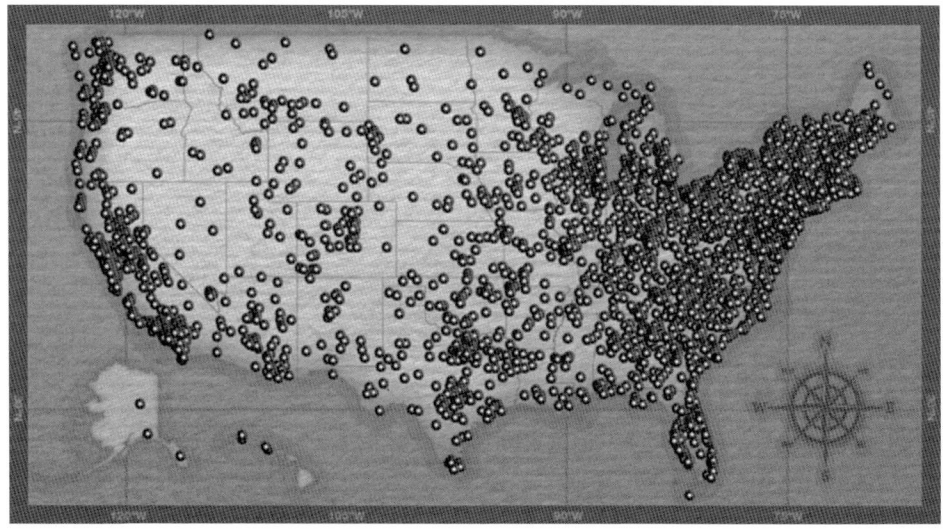

Search for your hometown history, your old stomping grounds, and even your favorite sports team.

Consistent with our mission to preserve history on a local level, this book was printed in South Carolina on American-made paper and manufactured entirely in the United States. Products carrying the accredited Forest Stewardship Council (FSC) label are printed on 100 percent FSC-certified paper.

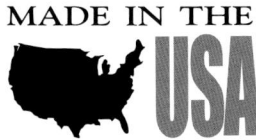